TO:

_____

FROM:

_____

The Heavens: Intimate Moments with Your Majestic God
© 2011 by Kevin Hartnett

Published in Nashville, Tennessee, by Thomas Nelson®. Thomas Nelson is a trademark of Thomas Nelson, Inc.
The Author is represented by and this book is published in association with the literary agency of WordServe Literary Group, Ltd., www.wordserveliterary.com.

Cover and interior design by Koechel Peterson Design, Minneapolis, MN.

Managing Editor: Lisa Stilwell

Thomas Nelson, Inc., titles may be purchased in bulk for educational, business, fund-raising, or sales promotional use. For information, please e-mail SpecialMarkets@ThomasNelson.com.

Unless otherwise noted, Scripture quotations are taken from THE NEW KING JAMES VERSION. © 1982 by Thomas Nelson, Inc. used by permission. All rights reserved.

Scripture quotations marked ESV are from THE ENGLISH STANDARD VERSION. © 2001 by Crossway Bibles, a division of Good News Publishers. RSV are from REVISED STANDARD VERSION of the Bible. © 1946, 1952, 1971, 1973 by the Division of Christian Education of the National Council of the Churches of Christ in the U.S.A. used by permission. NIV are from HOLY BIBLE:NEW INTERNATIONAL VERSION®. © 1973, 1978, 1984 by International Bible Society. Used by permission of Zondervan Publishing House. All rights reserved. NASB are from NEW AMERICAN STANDARD BIBLE®. © The Lockman Foundation 1960, 1962, 1963, 1968, 1971, 1972, 1973, 1975, 1977, 1995. Used by permission.

ISBN-13: 978-1-4041-8999-7

Printed in China

10 11 12 13 14 [RRD] 5 4 3 2 1

www.thomasnelson.com

THE
heavens
INTIMATE MOMENTS WITH
YOUR MAJESTIC GOD

BY KEVIN HARTNETT

Table of Contents

TABLE OF CONTENTS

Wonder & Worship

'Tis there, beyond the reach of Earth
That ever draws my heart away . . .
To wonder at the universe;
To think, to watch,
To dream, to pray.

There's nothing like gazing up into a dark, cloudless, star-filled sky to draw us into deeper communion with our Lord. He formed the universe in accordance with His greatness. It is unsearchably diverse, magnificently ordered, and astoundingly beautiful. On a journey begun years—even centuries—ago, starlight streams across the enormous expanse of space, revealing to us how the universe looked when it left its distant domain. There are strange and wonderful worlds out there: planets with impossibly high mountains, ring systems, and multiple moons; dense, colorful star clusters; and immense interstellar gas clouds. What new glories might we discover in these remote and mysterious havens!

But as beautiful and majestic as it is, the universe is groaning and longing—just as we are—for the completion of God's magnificent redemptive purpose in Christ (Romans 8:23). In towering grace, He plans to eradicate sin, reverse death, and create all things new. The new heavens and the new Earth will be even more glorious than what we see now. And our relationship with Him, who made all these things for His glory and our delight, will be one of endless, unhindered, joy-filled love.

Oh God, You are marvelous. No words can capture Your greatness. You are exalted in glory, yet intimate in care. Come back, Lord Jesus. Free us fully from the curse. Come back, Lord Jesus. Remove Your enemies and stretch time into eternity, as it cannot now contain the full measure of our praise. Come back, Lord Jesus. Set all things right, amen.

For we know that the whole creation groans and labors with birth pangs together until now. Not only that, but we also who have the firstfruits of the Spirit, even we ourselves groan within ourselves, eagerly waiting for the adoption, the redemption of our body.

Romans 8:22–23

BEAUTIFUL SATURN, QUEEN OF THE PLANETS, REVOLVES around the Sun outside the orbit of Jupiter, the planetary king of the solar system. Queen Saturn is the second largest planet. Its disk is about ten times the diameter of Earth. Though large, it is not as dense as Earth; rather, its density is less than that of water. If there were an ocean large enough to hold it, Saturn would float!

Stretching around the planet, however, is Saturn's most remarkable feature: a spectacular system of multibanded rings. Spectral analysis of the light reflected from these rings indicates that they are comprised primarily of bits of ice—millions of pieces that range in size from granules to house-sized chunks. The existence of the rings is somewhat of a mystery to astronomers; rings of this sort are usually unstable and will either collapse into the planet or disperse into space in a relatively short period of time. Yet Saturn's rings remain.

The simple but undeniable beauty of this lovely ringed orb points us to the ultimate source of all beauty, God Himself. We know about love because God is Love. We know about fatherhood because God is the Father. We know about beauty because God, the ultimate First Cause of everything, is also beautiful. As lovely as nature can be, its beauty is a distant and incomplete second to His. To the humble and worshipful of heart, every tiny jewel of creation brings to mind the magnificent Genius who fashioned it all. But no matter how dazzling, grand, or improbable, nothing in creation can compare to the infinite beauty of the Creator Himself. Praise Him for beauty as seen in all its forms, but worship Him alone as Beauty itself.

Honor and majesty are before Him;
Strength and beauty are in His sanctuary.

Psalm 96:6

Beauty

Beauty reaches through the eye,
To light upon a humble soul,
And teach this otherworldly truth:
No second piece conveys the Whole.

FAITH
AND
Patience

Certain seasons leave the heavens bare;
Others dazzle us with stars galore.
Take the lean in gratitude aware:
Times of deeper riches are in store.

I love those who love me,
And those who seek me diligently will find me.

Proverbs 8:17

IF YOU WERE TO COUNT THE NUMBER OF STARS VISIBLE TO THE naked eye on a typical night during each season of the year, you'd find that the totals vary significantly. Our disc-shaped solar system, located within a much larger disc-shaped spiral galaxy, is tipped at an angle of about sixty degrees with respect to our galaxy. What this means is that during the winter and summer months, we look out along the plane (the longer side) of the galaxy where there are more and brighter stars to be seen. In these seasons, the skies are brighter than in the spring and autumn months, when our line of sight is oriented "out the side" of the galaxy. This is one reason why the winter skies appear so brilliant, especially when compared to the humid, barren spring sky. It naturally follows, however, that more external galaxies can be seen during the spring and autumn months. At those times, it's easier to look past all the stars, dust, and gas of our galaxy to see the faint but glorious systems outside it.

Just as the seasons of bright constellations vary, so do the seasons of our experience with God's Word. In some weeks, our souls see bright, plain truths, and we revel in the wonderful sense of God's nearness, love, and care. At other times, it just doesn't seem like there's as much to see, and the Word—like the spring sky—seems a bit dull. Don't be discouraged. Ask the Spirit to reveal Christ to you; He will answer this prayer. Like the faint but marvelous spring-time galaxies, there are rich, deeper truths that wait for you to find them. Be patient in faith, with diligence for the Word to come alive to you in ways you haven't imagined.

And we desire that each one of you show the same diligence to
the full assurance of hope until the end,
that you do not become sluggish, but imitate those who
through faith and patience inherit the promises.

Hebrews 6:11–12

Jesus, the Cupbearer

Christ, the Humble, we adore You,
Son Eternal, sent to save;
Grasping not to heaven's glory;
Prince of Life, placed in a grave!
Well might brilliant angels marvel;
Devils, too, not comprehend:
Christ, Transcendent Praise of Heaven,
Sacrificed for sinful men!

ESO

There are eighty-eight constellations universally recognized by today's astronomers. Among these, only twelve (actually thirteen the way the constellation lines are now drawn) ever contain the Sun, Moon, and planets. These are the twelve well-known zodiac constellations, a name derived from a root word meaning "zoo." In the zoo are some familiar animals: Cancer the crab, Taurus the bull, Capricorn the goat, Leo the lion, Scorpio the scorpion, and Pisces the fish. Also on this special list are Libra the scales, Sagittarius the Centaur archer (half horse, half man), and four humans—the Gemini twins, Virgo the maiden, and last of all Aquarius the water bearer, or cupbearer.

The constellation of Aquarius is amongst the oldest known, probably because the winter solstice (the shortest day of the year) took place when the Sun was in Aquarius during the Early Bronze Age (beginning around 3000 BC). Interestingly, the ancient Sumerians associated the water bearer with the story of a global flood. Today, though, the idea of a water bearer or cupbearer brings to mind a servant. And when we as Christians think of servants, our minds naturally turn to Jesus. In Philippians 2:6–7, we're told that "though he was in the form of God, did not count equality with God a thing to be grasped, but made himself nothing, taking the form of a servant, being born in the likeness of men" (ESV). He came, as He said himself, "not to be served but to serve" (Mark 10:45 ESV). We recall how He washed the apostles' feet at the Last Supper, stating clearly that they should follow His example of humility.

Though we can and should imitate Him as a servant water bearer, in God's mercy we need not follow Him as cupbearer. It was Jesus alone who took the cup of God's righteous wrath for sins and drained it to the dregs at Calvary. When we hold the communion cup, we solemnly but joyfully remember Jesus' words: "For this is my blood of the covenant, which is poured out for many for the forgiveness of sins" (Matthew 26:28 ESV).

Thank You, Lord Jesus, for Your life and example of humility. Thank You for shedding Your blood for our sins. Fill me today with Your Spirit to be like You in humility and to serve others with my life. In Your name, for Your glory, I pray, amen.

"For even the Son of Man did not come to be served, but to serve, and to give His life a ransom for many."

Mark 10:45

NAMED AFTER ITS CODISCOVERERS, ALAN HALE AND Thomas Bopp, the magnificent Comet Hale-Bopp was easy to see with the naked eye during the months of March and April in 1997. Comets are bodies of dirty ice and rock that travel around the Sun in long elliptically shaped orbits. Some, like Comet Halley, return with relative frequency. But most comets (like Hale-Bopp) take thousands of years to complete just one trip around the Sun. Based on its orbit, this celestial visitor was last seen around the era of the Old Testament Patriarchs (circa 2000 BC). Because of their unpredictable appearances and motions, comets have been viewed by many cultures throughout history as heralds of doom. The English word *disaster* literally means "bad star," from the Greek *aster*.

Has a dirty ice ball of unpredicted and unwelcomed events careened into your life? Do circumstances seem completely haphazard or out of control? Are you fearful of what tomorrow might bring? If so, then be comforted by the knowledge that God is sovereign over all. Nothing is haphazard in His universe or beyond His control. Try to imagine the magnificent mind of God, working every circumstance—even the horrible death of His own Son on the cross—for the good of His sons and daughters. His timing may be beyond our comprehension, but trust that He has a grand design for your life.

And we know that all things work together for good to those who love God, to those who are the called according to His purpose.

Romans 8:28

Sovereignty

Minister of mystery,
The comet pierces history
And lifts the head of mortal mind
To contemplate the Grand Design.

GOD
Everlasting

When you fear you won't keep faith,
Trust God, the Everlasting.
When your weaknesses loom great,
Trust God, the Everlasting.
He spread out the heavens right,
Working wisdom, knowledge, might;
He will help you in your plight.
Trust God, the Everlasting.

Abraham planted a tamarisk tree in Beersheba and called there on the name of the Lord, the Everlasting God. And Abraham sojourned many days in the land of the Philistines.

Genesis 21:33–34 ESV

GOD HAS MANY NAMES IN HIS WORD. THE LARGE NUMBER OF THEM tells us that God delights in revealing Himself to us. Many of the Old Testament names are variations of *Jehovah* (meaning "I AM" or "pre-existent") or *El* (meaning "might," "strength," and "power"). *Jehovah* and *El* are often combined with other words to give us a greater understanding of the nature of our Lord.

One such combination is *El Olam*. *Olam* means "everlasting," so that together *El Olam* means "might everlasting," "strength everlasting," and "power everlasting." That is our God.

In Genesis 21:33, Abraham called upon *El Olam* to help him keep his commitments and to protect him from the dishonesty of others. In Isaiah 26:4, Isaiah encouraged his countrymen to trust in *El Olam* to keep and establish the nation of Judah. The prophet Jeremiah used the name to compare the unmatched power of the Lord who made the heavens to the impotency of man-made gods of wood and metal. "The gods who did not make the heavens and the earth shall perish from the earth and from under the heavens. It is he who made the earth by his power, who established the world by his wisdom, and by his understanding stretched out the heavens" (Jeremiah 10:11–12 ESV).

The same power, wisdom, and understanding that established the heavens are available to you. Are you worrying over your ability to keep a commitment you have made? Or do you worry that someone else will not keep their end of a deal? *El Olam* would have you place your trust in Him today—not the man-made idols of earthly security. He who spread out the heavens can equally work His power, wisdom, and understanding to help you in the situations you face. Call upon the God Everlasting. Call upon Him now.

You will keep him in perfect peace,
Whose mind is stayed on You,
Because he trusts in You.
Trust in the Lord forever,
For in YAH, the Lord, is everlasting strength.

Isaiah 26:3–4

Honoring God
& Giving Thanks

O God, what glories do I daily rob from You,
Knowing it's created things that I pursue
Rather than the One who caused all things to be?
Today, my loving Lord—and for eternity—
I choose to honor You and give You thanks.

In the book of Romans, the apostle Paul lays out an amazing doctrinal and practical discourse. In it he covers a lot of theological ground. His topics include the spiritual history of man, man's relationship to the law of God, man's dire state of unrighteousness because of sin, God's gracious redemption through faith in Christ, and how a person made alive in Christ should think and act with other believers. Paul argues that creation itself teaches us that a Being with a divine nature and eternal power created all that we see. Nowhere is this more gloriously evident than in the heavens. There we begin to grasp what eternity means—as immense, majestic galaxies, each filled with billions of stars, are seen in such vast numbers and at such great distances that all meaningful numbering and measuring systems begin to break down.

Seeing these evidences of a Supreme Being, men are without excuse if they choose to dishonor Him by worshiping created things rather than the Creator Himself. But Scripture also indicts man on a second count. That is, upon seeing creation, we sin not only for failing to honor God but for failing to give Him thanks. Have you ever thanked the Lord for creation? Does not creation teach us about His nature? Does it not thrill our souls with its beauty and humble us in its inexhaustible diversity? Do not the Sun, Moon, and stars serve us by forming the daily rhythms of our lives; graciously given to us by God for "signs and seasons, and for days and years" (Genesis 1:14)?

Today, let us take time to give Him thanks. As the Scriptures make clear, He's not only interested in our worship, but also in our gratitude. Tell Him what part of nature you like the most. Tell Him how you enjoy sunsets, waterfalls, clouds, trees, the beach, and the night sky. Thank Him for giving us these things to enjoy and to draw us closer to Him. Thank Him, finally, for being not only powerful but also personal.

For his invisible attributes, namely, his eternal power and divine nature, have been clearly perceived, ever since the creation of the world, in the things that have been made. So they are without excuse. For although they knew God, they did not honor him as God or give thanks to him, but they became futile in their thinking, and their foolish hearts were darkened.

Romans 1:20–21 ESV

PERHAPS TODAY YOU FIND YOURSELF SO EXHAUSTED AND disillusioned that you doubt whether God even sees or hears you. If so, God has a word for you. He has graciously written it down so you won't lose it. It's in Isaiah 40—*wait.*

It doesn't explain why everything is happening the way it is in your life, though you probably couldn't grasp God's perspective on it all anyway. But it does give you the path to hope, strength, and renewal; it is worshipful waiting. God invites you to count the stars in this image if you can—one small part of one star cluster, like hundreds of others in our galaxy alone, multiplied hundreds of times over in literally billions of other galaxies in the universe. He knows them all; He's named them all; He keeps them all—and He's not tired.

Waiting and trusting greatly honors the Lord, and He requires it from all His saints. It makes plain who's really the everlasting God and who rightly deserves praise. Pick any godly figure in the Scriptures and see how his or her power was "made perfect in weakness" (2 Corinthians 12:9). There's "a time for every purpose under heaven" (Ecclesiastes 3:1). Wait for His time, and until it comes, lift up your heart in worship and be renewed in Him.

Lift up your eyes on high, and see who has created these things, who brings out their host by number; He calls them all by name, by the greatness of His might and the strength of His power; not one is missing. Why do you say, O Jacob, and speak, O Israel: "My way is hidden from the L*ORD*, *and my just claim is passed over by my God"? Have you not known? Have you not heard? The everlasting God, the* L*ORD*, *the Creator of the ends of the earth, neither faints nor is weary. His understanding is unsearchable. He gives power to the weak, and to those who have no might He increases strength. Even the youths shall faint and be weary, and the young men shall utterly fall, but those who wait on the* L*ORD shall renew their strength; they shall mount up with wings like eagles, they shall run and not be weary, they shall walk and not faint.*

Isaiah 40:26–31

Needing Strength?

"How can it be," the Master said,
"I call the stars, but know not thee?
Think not, My way is hid from God,
My strength is theirs who wait for Me."

THE
Heavens
DECLARE

Dazzling phosphor in the night,
Silent orator, so bright,
How I marvel at your story
And the Hand behind your glory.

THE EXQUISITE STAR SIRIUS IS THE PREMIER GEM OF OUR SPARKLING winter skies. Its name means "the Sparkling or Scorching One," although it is also commonly called the Dog Star because of its location in the constellation of Canis Major, the Big Dog. Sirius is the brightest star visible from Earth (except, of course, for the Sun). This is due in part to its "nearby" location. Sirius is a mere 8.6 light-years distant from the solar system. That's the distance a light beam would travel in 8.6 years at the speed of 186,282 miles per second—about 50 trillion miles! Through careful study, astronomers have concluded that Sirius is about twice as massive as the Sun but about twenty-five times more luminous. This makes it a whopping 660,000 times more massive than Earth! It has a tiny companion star, no larger than Earth, called the "Pup," which is a white dwarf star. More than a hundred times smaller than the Sun, it has nearly the same mass, making it extraordinarily dense. A single teaspoon of its material would weigh more than fifteen hundred tons!

Psalm 19 tells us that the heavens declare the glory of God. Take any spot in the sky, and see that this is so. Whether we gaze upon stars, planets, galaxies, or nebulae, day after day and night after night they speak in loud, eloquent tongues of His power, knowledge, beauty, and glory. The Psalm says: "There is no speech, nor are there words"—what words could ever adequately describe His glory? "Yet their voice goes out through all the earth"—and results in the echoes of praise from men and women, great and small, old and young, from every nation, on every continent, in every age. Indeed, the starry heavens are declaring at this very moment that our God is magnificent beyond comprehension. Listen to them! Hear how their endless hosts strive day after day and night after night to declare the least part, the smallest measure, of His great glory. It is never enough; it never will be; it never can be. He is infinite. Have you heard their voices? Have you joined their chorus?

The heavens are telling the glory of God; and the firmament proclaims his handiwork. Day to day pours forth speech, and night to night declares knowledge. There is no speech, nor are there words; their voice is not heard; yet their voice goes out through all the earth, and their words to the end of the world.

Psalm 19:1–4 RSV

Sovereign King
AND
Caring Lord

O LORD, *how manifold are Your works!*
In wisdom You have made them all.

Psalm 104:24

ESO/J. Emerson/VISTA. Acknowledgment: Cambridge Astronomical Survey Unit

He reigns in distant realms of space,
Where whirling galaxies abound.

He governs every molecule
That quivers whispered words to sound.

He calls in place the bravest waves
Who hurl themselves to land from sea.

His seal impressed the continents;
He orders all majestically.

He hears the kidling on the crag,
Directing sunlight warm its way.

He sends the spring and autumn showers,
For which the flowered valleys pray.

He satisfies each varied kind
Of all creation, great and small.

His Word sustains the sum of them;
In faithfulness, He rules them all.

Oh, give Him praise with full accord,
This sovereign King and caring Lord,

Who caused in time the worlds that be,
Yet calls man to eternity.

His grace shall ever be explored;
His glory fills both earth and sky.

To Him your worship rightly bring
Your tongue, His Name, to magnify.

IF YOU'VE EVER TRIED TO REMOVE A SPOT FROM A DRESS OR PAIR OF pants, you know how stubborn even small ones can be. Thankfully, we're not charged with removing the spots from the Sun, for oftentimes, they're as large as (or even larger) than Earth itself!

Sunspots are magnetic storms that cause places on the Sun's surface to be cooler than the area surrounding them. They are actually brighter than a welder's arc but appear dark in contrast to the more dazzling and hotter surface of the Sun. The number of sunspots present on the Sun varies over an eleven-year period. Early in the cycle, they appear above and below the Sun's equator. As the cycle progresses and the number of spots increases, they are found closer and closer to the equator. Gradually, the numbers drop off, and the cycle starts again. Scientists have developed computer models that link this pattern to even longer cycle of magnetic field phenomena within the Sun.

Each of us has stubborn sins that spot our souls. As we try to rid ourselves of our particular tendencies, it can be helpful to look for cycles when these occur. We're deeply relational beings. Godless judgments about life made in reaction to people who have hurt us can predispose us toward fear, pride, or shame. Unthinkingly, we can be drawn into the sinful cycle of our own weaknesses—acting in self-pity, withdrawing from others, or perhaps even getting angry and attacking—as we reflexively crave the emotional satisfaction that only God can give us. You might call this "functional idolatry."

But when we choose to anchor ourselves in the gospel, we gain the deep satisfaction that we are "accepted in the Beloved" (Ephesians 1:6). We remember that God is our loving Father and we've been adopted into His family. We know that it is no longer us that lives but Christ that lives within us (Galatians 2:20). And daily we can learn to react as He would— forgiving the wrongs done to us by others, identifying and rejecting lies about God and others that lodge in our souls, filling our minds with the truth of God's Word, and glorifying God as our true source of joy. We can also sincerely repent, trusting in the promise of His gracious forgiveness through Christ to wash away all our sinful spots.

I am the LORD your God who brought you out of the land of Egypt, out of the house of bondage. You shall have no other gods before Me.

Deuteronomy 5:6–7

Spot Removal

Cyclic spots upon the soul
Show that lies have gained control.
Ask the Spirit where they be
Masking your idolatry.

⁓

NASA/Goddard Space Flight Center Scientific Visualization Studio

Praise

Tiny flickers overhead,
Torches from a thousand ages;
Now at length your work is done,
In my heart igniting praises.

He counts the number of the stars;
He calls them all by name.
Great is our LORD, and mighty in power;
His understanding is infinite.

Psalm 147:4–5

BEST SEEN FROM A DARK LOCATION ON LATE SUMMER NIGHTS IN THE Northern Hemisphere, the magnificent glowing band called the Milky Way stretches majestically from horizon to horizon. This view shows a small section of the Milky Way, north of the prominent constellation Cygnus the Swan. While the band simply appears as a white, knotty glow to the naked eye, it actually contains millions upon millions of individual stars. These stars, as well as our own star, the Sun, are all part of an immense pinwheel-shaped spiral system known as the Milky Way Galaxy. Astronomers estimate that at least 200 billion stars populate the galaxy.

The bright star to the right in the photo is called Deneb, an ancient name meaning "tail," as it marks the tail of the Swan. It is one of the most luminous stars in the sky. Fully 60,000 times more luminous than the Sun, this star is estimated to be nearly sixteen hundred light-years away—that's 9.6 thousand trillion miles! If it were as close to Earth as the bright winter star Sirius, it would rival the full moon in brightness. The reddish cloud next to Deneb is a glowing cloud of ionized hydrogen called the North American Nebula.

It is a cause of great wonder that these immense, intensely brilliant stars are so distant that they appear only as dim pinpricks of light. Equally amazing is that since light travels at a finite speed across the vast expanses of the galaxy, their starlight carries information about how things looked in the past, not the present. At sixteen hundred light-years away, Deneb's light left the star sixteen hundred years ago—during the time the Visigoths were sacking Rome!

The heavens declare God's glory. That is why He presents them to us. They show Him to be Lord over time and space. He is powerful, majestic, infinite, and creative beyond measure. The heavens declare these things better than anything else in all the created order. Contemplate the Maker of heaven and Earth today, and let His works ignite praise in your soul.

GOD'S WORD ASSURES US THAT HIS MERCIES ARE NEW EVERY morning. This is a wonderful promise, but only because we know tomorrow is but hours away. It would not be so if we lived elsewhere in the solar system. The lengths of the day and night on a planet are set by how fast it rotates into and out of the sunlight. These speeds vary widely. Because of its slow rotation and rapid movement around the Sun, the interval between one sunrise and the next on Mercury is 176 Earth days! Pluto's day is about the same length as six Earth days, but it spins in the opposite direction. The Sun rises in the west and sets in the east there. The giant planet Jupiter has the shortest day—just under ten Earth hours. You could sleep all night on Jupiter and only log about five hours of rest! But the strangest place for calendars and clocks in the solar system is on the planet Venus. The Venusian day is longer than its year! It laps completely around the Sun before it can even spin once on its axis. A year on Venus is about 225 Earth days; yet a single day is 243. It also spins in the opposite direction from the Earth, so the Sun rises in the west there too, as on Pluto and Uranus.

God created the lights in the heavens for "signs and seasons, and for days and years" (Genesis 1:14). He did this in wisdom and kindness. If we have a bad day, a new and different one will begin in just a few hours. Our weeks, months, seasons, and years also put rhythms into our lives that help us focus and be fruitful. And as faithful as the sunrise, God is faithful in the execution of His promises to us. Though we have trials, in the midst of them He delivers, protects, strengthens, and provides. "Weeping may tarry for the night, but joy comes with the morning" (Psalm 30:5 ESV).

But this I call to mind,

and therefore I have hope:

The steadfast love of the LORD never ceases;

his mercies never come to an end;

they are new every morning;

great is your faithfulness.

Lamentations 3:21–23 ESV

Mercy &
Faithfulness

Today, God's mercy rises with the sunshine;
Our darkened globe spins gladly to His face.
Take heart, my soul, your puny clouds of doubting
Can't stop the dawn, nor Faithfulness displace.

Where Is Heaven?

Heaven is an actual place,
Not just a state of mind.
We might see it out in space,
But will more likely find
The universe has doorways
Where angels come and go,
As scientists explore ways
Our four dimensions grow.

WHERE PRECISELY IS HEAVEN? IS IT A REAL PLACE? WILL ASTRONOMERS FIND it with their telescopes? These are great questions, and only one has a very good answer at present: the *new* heavens and the new Earth will most assuredly be real, physical places—perhaps more accurately one place where the two are blended together—but they won't be created until after Christ returns, so they certainly can't be seen now. The whole tone of Scripture declares that they will be physical, not immaterial. God in Christ is working out a tremendous redemptive plan that frees our present physical creation from the curse, abolishes death, and restores all things to their "very good" state prior to the Fall. The precise nature of the new order is blessedly beyond our ability to fully grasp, but it will no doubt include familiar elements of our current creation transformed into their perfect, more glorious versions.

But what of the intermediate place or places where departed souls await the Last Day, the final judgment, and the making of all things new? Is this a physical place in the four dimensional space-time continuum of the universe? Perhaps, since Christ's resurrected body had definite physical characteristics. But it is also possible that it exists in the universe, but in a different dimension within it.

Particle physicists see very startling behavior from matter at the atomic level. Elementary particles seem to pop in and out of existence in ways that simply aren't understood. It's almost as if they pass in and out of a different dimension. Similarly, astronomers are wrestling with evidence that the universe is filled with a different kind of matter and energy that can't be found in the laboratory but that appear to effect the movement and distribution of galaxies.

So, just as Jesus in His glorified body was able to transcend the normally understood limitations of matter, and just as angels appeared to move from physical to nonphysical states, so too we may meet the Lord in a different dimension and wait until He creates all things new. Until then, we have His solemn assurance that He is preparing a place for us.

"Let not your heart be troubled; you believe in God, believe also in Me. In My Father's house are many mansions; if it were not so, I would have told you. I go to prepare a place for you. And if I go and prepare a place for you, I will come again and receive you to Myself; that where I am, there you may be also."

John 14:1–3

God
Omniscient

He knows the name of every star in heaven;
He knows when sparrows light upon the ground.
Of every atom brought into Creation,
His full and caring knowledge is profound.

GOD'S KNOWLEDGE IS PROFOUND—PROFOUND BEYOND GRASPING OR describing. Indeed, finding words to capture and communicate even a fraction of His omniscience is a pitiful exercise. He knows *everything*. Everything that ever was, everything that currently exists, everything that ever will be. He knows all about it. Its history, its parts, its dimensions, its workings. He knows what might have been. He knows what could have been. He knows what ought to have been. He knows forces and motives, reasons and rationales, desires and goals. These things completely defy our understanding.

To help us glimpse His greatness, the Lord has given us the heavens. See how they declare His glory. Galaxy upon galaxy, as far as our telescopes can see, speckle the night sky. Each one has countless stars and multitudes of planets and moons. Each one has its own history, conditions, features, and futures—and God knows everything about them all. And if these countless "known" galaxies weren't enough, Hubble images like this one reveal galaxies beyond the galaxies—strange, arc-shaped streaks of light bent into view by the gravity of intervening galaxies.

In Matthew 10:29–30, Jesus reminds us that God keeps track of even the seemingly insignificant things—like the sparrows that were sold two for a penny at the temple. He assures us that we are of much greater value to Him than they. Take Him at His word. Humbly believe that He knows everything about you and your situation—even the number of hairs on your head—and commit yourself to His care.

> *To whom then will you compare me,*
> *that I should be like him? says the Holy One.*
> *Lift up your eyes on high and see:*
> *who created these?*
> *He who brings out their host by number,*
> *calling them all by name,*
> *by the greatness of his might,*
> *and because he is strong in power*
> *not one is missing.*

Isaiah 40:25–26 ESV

As for God, His way is perfect;
The word of the LORD is proven;
He is a shield to all who trust in Him.

2 Samuel 22:31

HOW BEAUTIFUL AND QUIETLY IMPORTANT IS OUR NEAREST celestial neighbor, the Moon. From the thin, smiling crescent phase, to the round, dazzlingly bright full Moon, the Earth's only natural satellite magnificently adorns the night sky. It is the object of both our interest and our romance. In Genesis 1:16, it is described as the "lesser light to rule the night," and indeed it guides the affairs of men and animals alike. It has been used to establish calendars, set military engagements, and assist in navigation. The Moon's gravity directs the daily ebb and flow of the ocean's tides, which in turn affect many species of plants and animals. But a lesser known trait of the Moon is that it helps stabilize the Earth's axis of rotation. Without the Moon nearby, the Earth would wobble under the gravitational influence of the other planets, causing more severe seasons and dramatic climate changes.

Have you ever prayed for God's protection? How do you suppose He's answered? Sometimes the answers are obvious: a near miss from a car accident or a failed business deal that you later learn would have been disastrous to you or your company. Imagine the sheer number of these occurrences! Today, let us thank God for His protection in all the many ways we both see and don't see: our amazing immune systems, our homes, our clothing, the atmosphere that protects us from cosmic rays, the governing laws of physics themselves—and, yes, the Moon, as it quietly and consistently brings stability to our weather. As you peer up at the Moon, this "ruler of the night," listen as she reminds you to pause, think, and worship the God who so thoughtfully ordered it all.

But let all who take refuge in you rejoice;
let them ever sing for joy,
and spread your protection over them,
that those who love your name may exult in you.

Psalm 5:11 ESV

GOD'S PROTECTION

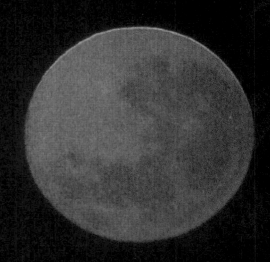

The lesser light, which rules the night,
Imparts to me this one decree:
When I arise, consider me.

In the book of Revelation, we're given a preview of truly astonishing things to come. Powerful angelic beings are seen carrying out God's end-time purposes on Earth. There are four "living creatures" (4:6), each with six wings, full of eyes all around forever calling "Holy, holy, holy, is the Lord God Almighty" (v. 8 ESV). There is the throne, surrounded by a rainbow that has the appearance of jasper. In front of the throne there is "as it were a sea of glass, like crystal" (v. 6 ESV). There are elders and crowns, lightning and thunder, torches and trumpets.

And as the apostle John wrestles to convey the wonder and majesty of everything he's privileged to see, we're told something completely amazing that in context almost seems like an aside: "And night will be no more" (22:5 ESV). What? No more starry nights? No more full moons or lunar eclipses? No more glorious galaxies to view with our telescopes? Apparently not, at least not in the way we know them now. We read that the stars "fell to the earth, as a fig tree drops its late figs when it is shaken by a mighty wind. Then the sky receded as a scroll when it is rolled up"(6:13–14). Amazing! He who spoke it all into existence with a word will roll it up like a scroll!

Will this be cause for sorrow? Not in the least. For the apostle then goes on to say: "Now I saw a new heaven and a new earth, for the first heaven and the first earth had passed away. Also there was no more sea. Then I, John, saw the holy city, New Jerusalem, coming down out of heaven from God, prepared as a bride adorned for her husband. And I heard a loud voice from heaven saying, 'Behold, the tabernacle of God is with men, and He will dwell with them, and they shall be His people. God Himself will be with them and be their God. And God will wipe away every tear from their eyes; there shall be no more death, nor sorrow, nor crying. There shall be no more pain, for the former things have passed away.' Then He who sat on the throne said, 'Behold, I make all things new'" (21:1–5).

There will no doubt be elements of the old order in the new, as He will redeem the original creation—but they will be perfected. The glories of the new heaven and the new earth will completely defy all imagination and description. Let us worship Him today for the current order but also yearn in faith for His indescribable return.

There shall be no night there: They need no lamp nor light of the sun, for the Lord God gives them light. And they shall reign forever and ever.

Revelation 22:5

E. Jehin and A. Correa, (ESO)

No More Night

There'll come a Day that knows no end,
A time when Night shall be no more.
A Day no dawn, nor dusk, attend,
When stars aren't needed anymore.
For God Himself will be our light;
No lamp, nor Sun that day there'll be.
He'll remake then for our delight
The heavens more fantastically.

Phosphors IN THE Cosmos

Phosphors in the cosmos,
We are called to be;
Lights into the darkness,
Meant for all to see.
Given not to grumbling,
Innocent of hate,
Children of the Father,
Boldly shining straight.

Only let your manner of life be worthy of the gospel of Christ.

Philippians 1:27 ESV

DO YOU KNOW SOMEONE WHO IS ALWAYS CHEERFUL AND HELPFUL? What about someone who's always grumpy and complaining? There's a world of difference between the two! No doubt we're attracted to the first and seek to avoid the second. God calls us to be in the first category: good listeners, cheerful, and humbly ready to help others—even if (and when) we're inconvenienced. These character qualities blaze forth like shining lights into the darkened lives of those around us and give much glory to God. One translation describes the effect of such individuals as "lights in the world" (Philippians 2:15 ESV). Another translates the text as "stars in the sky" (NIV). The Greek words themselves are transliterated "phosphors in the cosmos"—an utterly beautiful and compelling picture of dazzling lives, whether by day or by night.

But how can one be this way all the time? It's so unnatural! The answer is provided in the same passage: "holding fast to the word of life" (v. 16 ESV). No matter what problems you are facing today, if you're a Christian, God has already solved your biggest problem. You who were dead He made alive in Christ through the gospel (Ephesians 2:5). You have been reconciled to God and can now relate to Him as Father, not Judge. Your eternal life has been secured once and for all by Christ Himself, who will never leave nor forsake you.

If this can't make us cheerful, what can? May the Lord open the eyes of our understanding today, that we might walk in a manner that is worthy of our calling.

Do all things without grumbling or questioning, that you may be blameless and innocent, children of God without blemish in the midst of a crooked and twisted generation, among whom you shine as lights in the world, holding fast to the word of life.

Philippians 2:14–16 ESV

41

THE TWO BRIGHTEST OBJECTS IN OUR NIGHTTIME SKY, THE Moon and the planet Venus, combined their brilliance for this spectacular sight on the morning of January 27, 1995. Although not rare, optical co-alignments like this of Venus and the Moon (called *conjunctions*) usually happen only a couple times a year, and they're easy to miss unless you're watchful.

Scripture tells us that true disciples of Christ are born from above, created for good works that God prepares in advance for us to do (Ephesians 2:10). Most likely these works will involve others. The Lord has placed someone in our lives this very day to whom He wants us to serve in some way. Maybe it will simply be to bless with kindness, support, encouragement, or prayer. And perhaps, in God's sovereignty, it may lead to something much more.

Jesus chanced to meet a woman at a well, and it resulted in a citywide revival. Philip met an Ethiopian eunuch who was ripe to receive the good news and, as a result, the word of Christ spread to his country. Paul met a demon-possessed woman in Philippi and, by helping her, landed in prison—where he was used by God to preach to the jailor. What divinely appointed conjunction will we make today? Whose life will we touch? A family member? Coworker? Neighbor? There may even be a complete stranger who comes across our path today that God intends for us to bless. In light of all of this, let us in faith commit ourselves to be watchful.

For we are His workmanship, created in Christ Jesus for good works, which God prepared beforehand that we should walk in them.

Ephesians 2:10

Kevin Hottnett

Sovereignty
AND
Conjunction

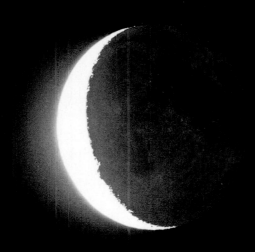

If, by chance, a random meeting waxes great,
Quickly stop and ask the Spirit whether
He who orders everything in time and space
Hasn't planned to bring you two together.

Hallowed
Be Thy Name

All Your works shall praise You, O Lord,
And Your saints shall bless You.
They shall speak of the glory of Your kingdom,
And talk of Your power,
To make known to the sons of men His mighty acts,
And the glorious majesty of His kingdom.
Your kingdom is an everlasting kingdom,
And Your dominion endures throughout all generations.

Psalm 145:10–13

For Your genius in creation,
Hallowed be Thy Name!
Power shown to ev'ry nation,
Hallowed be Thy Name!

For dominions great and small,
Molecules and starry skies,
Order brought to unseen reaches . . .
Hallowed, hallowed be Thy Name!

For Your wisdom ruling hist'ry,
Hallowed be Thy Name!
Righteous judgments, gracious purpose,
Hallowed be Thy Name!

For the people that You chose;
Laws exposing human need;
Prophecy and sure fulfillment . . .
Hallowed, hallowed be Thy Name!

For the wonder of the gospel,
Hallowed be Thy Name!
Christ the cursed, and we the pardoned!
Hallowed be Thy Name!

Triumph of Your Perfect Love—
Holiness and Peace embrace!
Now forever to the Lamb sing . . .
Hallowed, hallowed be Thy Name!

Solitude

If distractions form your daily diet,
Hurriedness the course to which you're prone,
Take a walk at night beneath the quiet.
Seek God's mercies, listening there alone.

WE ALL HAVE INCREASINGLY BUSY LIVES, AND LIFE IN THE "INFORMATION age" only seems to pick up pace. Less frequent landline telephone calls and "snail mail" letters have given way to a daily barrage of texts and twitters. If we miss our e-mail for a day, the number of stacked-up messages looks like the arrival and departure board at the airport. Traffic rages around us daily, resulting in congestion and delays as everyone scrambles to live the "good life" filled with sports, concerts, church meetings, and family events. The kids need attention, the grandparents need attention, the bills need attention—the empty refrigerator, the car, the house, the yard, the garage, our clothes, our jobs, our bodies. Frequently we get to Wednesday of the work- or school week, and we'd swear it was Friday. Bedtime has never had so much appeal!

Our Lord understands. The gospel of Mark records that Jesus was so busy healing and teaching those who sought Him out that He didn't even have time to eat. His mother and brothers thought He was out of His mind. What did Jesus do? He pulled away. He withdrew when the Sun went down to be alone with His Father in prayer. Nighttime gives us a wonderful opportunity to do the same. Take a walk—or at least pull away from the daily grind—and have fellowship with your Maker, Savior, and Helper. If you can, go out beneath the Moon and stars. Think about how Jesus stared up at the very same ones as He prayed, and delight with Him in the discipline of solitude. He modeled its value for us in His own life on Earth. The same beautiful starry sky and gracious Father await us as did Him. Go experience them both.

"Come to Me, all you who labor and are heavy laden, and I will give you rest. Take My yoke upon you and learn from Me, for I am gentle and lowly in heart, and you will find rest for your souls. For My yoke is easy and My burden is light."

Matthew 11:28–30

ONE OF THE TITLES GIVEN TO JESUS IN THE BOOK OF REVELATION IS "THE Bright and Morning Star" (22:16). What does this mean? Those familiar with astronomy know that in virtually all months of the year, a brilliant "star" can be seen just after sunset, or just before sunrise. Those less knowledgeable about the sky may have heard the terms Morning Star and Evening Star, but not realized that they are one and the same object: the planet Venus.

The orbit of Venus is interior to Earth's, which means that no matter where we are in our orbit around the Sun (that is, no matter what time of year), one only has to look in the general direction of the Sun to see it. Since all the planets orbit the Sun in roughly the same plane, Venus appears to move back and forth across the sky in a relatively straight line. Over a period of weeks, Venus rises in the east (morning) until it reaches the point of its greatest "elongation" from the Sun. Then it begins—day by day—to descend to the horizon, reappearing in the western (evening) sky, where it repeats the pattern. The much smaller planet Mercury does the same thing. But being closer to the Sun than Venus, it stays very low to the horizon even at its highest point and is not nearly as bright. Venus is roughly the size of Earth, but it is perpetually covered with thick clouds. These clouds reflect the Sun's rays like a planet-sized white sheet, making Venus brilliantly bright—bright enough even to cast a shadow on Earth.

When we consider Jesus as the Morning Star, we contemplate His beauty and power as a foretaste of the fully realized kingdom of God. In His first coming, Jesus revealed in part the glory of the Godhead, which will not be completely manifested until He comes again in the clouds. In that day, "the heavens will pass away with a great noise, and the elements will melt with fervent heat; both the earth and the works that are in it will be burned up" (2 Peter 3:10). God will destroy the current order with fire and remake the heavens and the Earth in a fashion that defies description or comprehension.

Seeing the glorious morning star reminds us that the even more glorious Sun is just over the horizon—and that the Morning Star Himself is coming one day soon. Take heart today, whatever your circumstances, for He comes as assuredly as the dawn. "Behold, I am coming quickly, and My reward is with Me" (Revelation 22:12).

"I, Jesus, have sent my angel to testify to you about these things for the churches. I am the root and the descendant of David, the bright morning star."

Revelation 22:16 ESV

Christ,
THE MORNING STAR

Brilliant there with dawn ascending;
Glorious shines the morning star!
Brightness of the day portending,
See its face reflected far!
Signal that the night has ended,
Nature's call to greet the light.
Preview there the fire more splendid;
Shine, and let the day ignite!

For God, who said, "Let light
shine out of darkness," has shone
in our hearts to give the light of
the knowledge of the glory of God
in the face of Jesus Christ.

2 Corinthians 4:6 ESV

GOD SEES
ALL
ACCURATELY

Looking with the human eye
Can indeed the truth belie.
Let us with God's Word agree:
He Who formed the eye can see.

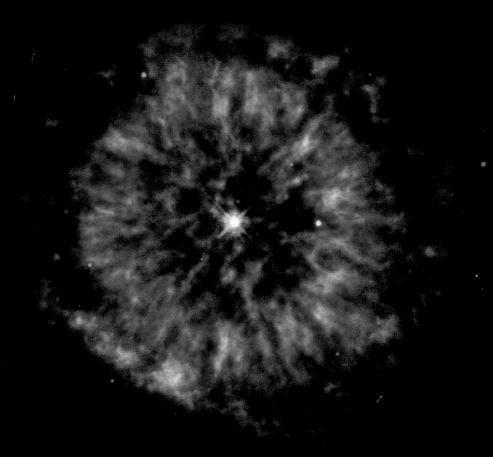

THIS BEAUTIFUL HUBBLE SPACE TELESCOPE IMAGE IS OF AN OBJECT catalogued as NGC 6751. In telescopes of lesser resolution, it looks amazingly like a gigantic eye staring back at you from space! Of course, the truth is not what it first appears to be. In reality, the disc of the "eye" is a huge, expanding envelope of gas released from the white star at its center. Objects like this are known to astronomers as *planetary nebulae*. This is because in the first telescopes to reveal them, they appeared as tiny discs, much like the distant solar system planets. Astronomers now find them all over the sky. Once thought to be only spherical, they are now seen to take many astounding and beautiful shapes. They are stars in the late stages of their lives, whose internal processes are out of balance. Much remains to be learned about these objects and why they spawn the shapes they do.

We can learn several lessons from these planetary nebulae, particularly this one. First, human perspective is flawed. We see things through the bias of our own understanding and experience, but both of these are limited. We must not rush to conclusions. Second, we shouldn't ascribe spiritual significance to natural things that happen to look like something religious—like seeing the face of Jesus in the sand or seeing God's eye in the heavens. Finally, we should steep ourselves in the Word of God to gain a proper perspective on all things, spiritual and natural. God sees everything with perfect accuracy; He designed the eye, after all! Let us learn to live in agreement with the truth as revealed in His Word.

Understand, O dullest of the people!
Fools, when will you be wise?
He who planted the ear, does he not hear?
He who formed the eye, does he not see?
He who disciplines the nations, does he not rebuke?
He who teaches man knowledge—
the LORD*—knows the thoughts of man,*
that they are but a breath.

Psalm 94:8–11 ESV

The constellation Leo the Lion shines prominently in the springtime sky for those living in the Northern Hemisphere. It is generally depicted as a lion lying in profile with its head up. The head has a very recognizable sickle shape that looks to modern generations like a backward question mark. The constellation has been associated with the figure of a lion by many different cultures from the dawn of civilization. It has also taken on the connotation of royalty—not only because the stately lion is universally seen as the king of the beasts, but also because 3,000 years ago, the Sun passed through Leo during the summer solstice (the longest day of the year), and the Sun was often considered a royal deity. Leo's brightest star, Regulus, even means "little king." Some believe that the mythological figure of the Sphinx (a lion's body with a human head) derived its shape from this constellation.

People of all ages and cultures have looked at this group of stars and been reminded both of a lion and of a reigning, conquering king. How fitting for us then to remember the "Lion of Judah," the Lord Jesus Christ. He was a descendant in the flesh of Judah, the son of Jacob. And in Genesis 49:9, we read how Jacob described Judah as a young lion and predicted that his descendants would rule over the other eleven tribes. King David and King Solomon were both descendants of Judah and great kings and conquerors. But no other man, king, or commoner, has conquered sin and lived a fully righteous life before God—only Jesus. He alone defeated the flesh and—on the cross—triumphed over the demonic principalities and powers that held souls captive and alienated from God (Colossians 2:15). Then He gloriously rose from the grave, conquering man's final enemy: death. There is no greater victory to be won, and no greater victor than our Lord Jesus. This is why for all eternity He will bear the name above every name: "King of kings and Lord of lords" (Revelation 19:16).

So I wept much, because no one was found worthy to open and read the scroll, or to look at it. But one of the elders said to me, "Do not weep. Behold, the Lion of the tribe of Judah, the Root of David, has prevailed to open the scroll and to loose its seven seals."

Revelation 5:4–5

The Lion of *Judah*

Jesus, Judah's conquering Son,
Earned great victories, ne'er outdone;
Hence His Name all heav'n records:
King of kings and Lord of lords.

God
Unchangeable

Change requires that good or bad be heightened;
Careful thought will tell you this is so.
Therefore those whose outlook is enlightened
Find their awe and worship only grow.

THEOLOGIANS FREQUENTLY CLASSIFY THE VARIOUS ATTRIBUTES OF GOD as *communicable* (ones that we share in part with the Lord) and *incommunicable* (ones that He possesses but we don't). Among His communicable attributes are love, truth, and wisdom—characteristics that we demonstrate, but not fully or purely. Among His incommunicable attributes are His eternal existence, His transcendence over time and space, and His unchangeableness.

James 1:17 teaches us that with God "there is no variation or shadow due to change" (ESV). God's being, His perfections, His purposes, and His promises do not change. We might be tempted to respond, "Okay, so what? What difference does that make in my life?" The answer: it can make a *profound* difference in the strength of your faith.

Think about this: if the character of God could change, it must necessarily change to become better (meaning He is not perfect now) or worse (meaning He is corruptible). If His character, His plans, intentions, and promises, aren't fully trustworthy and perfect now, why would we believe His Word or trust in His plan for salvation? No, God is unchangeable. He is perfect. We can trust that He won't take a different view of His saving grace tomorrow or change His promise that "all things work together for good to those who love God, to those who are the called according to His purpose" (Romans 8:28).

The heavens change, though very slowly. Jesus saw a slightly different shape to the constellation of Orion the Hunter than the one Abraham saw or the one we see now. But God's plans and promises do not change. Let's rejoice today that God is unchangeable and worship Him for His unchanging nature the next time we look up and consider the heavens.

Of old You laid the foundation of the earth,
And the heavens are the work of Your hands.
They will perish, but You will endure;
Yes, they will all grow old like a garment;
Like a cloak You will change them,
And they will be changed.
But You are the same,
And Your years will have no end.

Psalm 102:25–27

Kevin Hartnett

God
IN THE
Galaxy

Impossibly gigantic,
Yet hid from normal view,
With silent force controlling
The sum in your purview.
And is it not these likenesses,
In beauty, strength, and grace,
That take my eye to see in you
The Great Designer's trace?

To whom then will you liken God, or
what likeness compare with him?

Isaiah 40:18 ESV

THIS STUNNING IMAGE OF THE WHIRLPOOL GALAXY, M51, WAS taken by the Hubble Space Telescope from high in orbit—well above the blurring effects of Earth's atmosphere. It reveals in new detail the nature of the galaxy's sweeping spiral arms: immense structures of gas, dust, and clusters of stars curving through the emptiness of outer space. The size of this galaxy boggles the mind. If we were to reduce our own solar system of planets—billions of miles in diameter—down to the size of a cookie, M51 in proper scale would be larger than the continental United States! Spiral galaxies rotate everything in them in immense circular orbits that take millions of years to complete.

The attributes of God can be likened to a gigantic spiral galaxy. Both are too grand to fully comprehend. As huge as our own Milky Way Galaxy is, and despite the fact that it is silently hurling our entire solar system around its center at a speed faster than a bullet, we live completely unaware of its presence and influence. How similar this is to God! Every moment, our lives are silently guided by His powerful sovereignty, but we don't even know it. Then, too, behold the majesty and beauty of the galaxy's spectacular and mysterious spiral arms. All these things help us glimpse the Genius of creation Himself: God—the Great Designer of all.

Lord, there is no created thing, however grand or magnificent, that adequately compares with You. Thank You for the heavens, which reveal to us, in part, Your great glory. You are great and greatly to be praised, amen.

Yours, O LORD, is the greatness,
The power and the glory,
The victory and the majesty;
For all that is in heaven and in earth is Yours;
Yours is the kingdom, O LORD,
And You are exalted as head over all.

1 Chronicles 29:11

It was Sir Isaac Newton (1642–1727) who first derived the mathematical formulas that explain how gravity controls the motions of astronomical bodies. These formulas allow astronomers to accurately predict the locations of the solar system planets in the future, as well as in the past. Their orbits, including Earth's, are amazingly regular. This is why astronomers can confidently publish almanacs with the rising and setting times for the Sun and Moon, planets and stars. Einstein's Theory of Relativity further refined these equations, making the predictive power of the mathematics even greater. It wasn't until the advent of high-speed computers, however, that astronomers began to appreciate the more subtle gravitational interactions between astronomical bodies. These interactions form "resonances" that amplify tiny orbital differences and lead to zones where orbits are not stable and astronomical bodies cannot stay indefinitely. The rings of Saturn are examples; the resonances caused by Saturn's moons create gaps in the rings.

As we all know, life has both predictable and unpredictable elements. The peace—and stagnation—that comes with predictability the Lord lovingly punctuates with trials. These are designed to refine our faith and prove Him faithful. Scripture does, however, give us a way to view life with an overall sense of predictability. It's found in Ephesians 2. If you're a Christian, God has created you for good works, and He's prepared them in advance for you.

No matter what your circumstances, God has good works prepared for you to do each day. What might they look like? Service to a neighbor or coworker? Encouraging a member of your family or church? Giving generously to a godly cause? Teaching children to love and serve the Lord? Or perhaps praying—a good work that may rank higher than them all. Whatever the case, you can predict with certainty that there *will* be God's work to do and that the Spirit of God can help you see it and do it. Start living today in the adventure of seeking God's good works and walking in them.

For we are His workmanship, created
in Christ Jesus for good works, which
God prepared beforehand that we
should walk in them.

Ephesians 2:10

Predictability

Lord, I've found a new adventure,
Sensing what You'd have me do;
Daily finding Your good works means
All the glory goes to You.

PRAYING
for Lost Loved Ones

Gazing 'neath the starry skies
Abram heard the guarantee:
"Though you cannot sire a one,
So shall your descendants be."
Let us then look into heav'n,
Trusting God to hear our plea:
"Though we cannot sire a one,
Saved may our descendants be."

*But as many as received Him, to them He gave the right to
become children of God, to those who believe in His name:
who were born, not of blood, nor of the will of the flesh, nor
of the will of man, but of God.*

John 1:12–13

THIS BEAUTIFUL IMAGE IS OF THE STAR CLUSTER AND SURROUNDING NEBULA known to astronomers as NGC 602. It is located in the Small Magellanic Cloud, a small neighboring galaxy of the Milky Way. Along with the Large Magellanic Cloud, it is visible to the unaided eye in the night skies of the Southern Hemisphere, where they both appear as small, faint clouds. They were recorded by Middle Eastern astronomers as early as AD 964, but news of their existence wasn't recorded by Europeans until the late fifteenth century and then again in the early sixteenth century by the returning crew of Ferdinand Magellan's famous around-the-world voyage.

Most astronomers believe the stars in NGC 602 are relatively young, having formed from the surrounding molecular clouds. The details of this process are poorly understood. For clouds to collapse under the weight of their own gravity somehow requires them to overcome their own outward pressure. This pressure increases as the gases heat up. There are also theoretical problems with how angular momentum can be conserved in a collapsing cloud without producing a star that spins much more rapidly than any seen. Magnetic fields may play a role, but the whole picture of star birth defies easy explanation.

Much like this, the process of being born again also defies explanation. God's Spirit somehow illuminates our minds and hearts to reveal both our need for a savior and His remarkable provision in Christ. But why were we ourselves so dull to these truths for so long, and why are some of our loved ones—like parents or siblings—still so spiritually blind? This is a particular grief to those who have unbelieving descendants. Today let us renew our prayers for them. God is "mighty to save" (Isaiah 63:1) He was mighty to Abraham and Sarah, producing a whole nation from their aged bodies. God alone can accomplish the miracle of new birth. Let us then hold our unbelieving relatives before Him, pleading for Him to overcome all those natural forces that keep the fire of faith from igniting.

*When His disciples heard it, they were
greatly astonished, saying, "Who then can
be saved?" But Jesus looked at them and
said to them, "With men this is impossible,
but with God all things are possible."*

Matthew 19:25–26

The Different One

This we recognize as love:
You gave up Your throne above;
O make us this benevolent
With those who are so different.

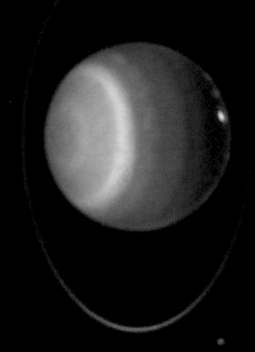

THE PLANETS OF OUR SOLAR SYSTEM ARE A DIVERSE LOT. SOME ARE LARGE and gaseous; some small and rocky; some spin quickly and others slowly; some have magnetic fields and some are without; some have many moons and others have none. But even with all their differences, one planet stands out as a true oddity: Uranus, the seventh planet from the Sun. To begin with, it rolls. While we might picture all the planets as spinning tops whose northern and southern poles all point approximately in the same direction—Uranus's doesn't. Its poles are where the other planets have their equators. Uranus is basically rolling around the solar system on its side. It's also spinning backward, so that the Sun rises in the west and sets in the east. Like Earth, Uranus has a magnetic field. But unlike Earth, it's not oriented north and south, nor even east and west. It's in between—about sixty degrees from its own north and south orientation. Its magnetic field–producing source is also not at its center but is instead shifted about one-third of the way to the surface on one side. Even the name *Uranus* is different, coming from Greek mythology, not Roman.

Do you know someone who is a bit of an oddity? Someone who is just . . . different? Perhaps they homeschool—or *don't* homeschool. Perhaps they dress unusually or love all the movies you hate. Maybe they enjoy a "weird" organic diet or celebrate the anniversaries of events you don't care about in the least. If so, the Lord has written a whole chapter in the Bible (Romans 14) about how we're to relate to them. In two words, it's this: *accept* and *love*. Not meaning to accept outright sinful behavior—but rather we accept those who are different from us by not passing judgment on their choices or convictions. If God has accepted someone, "Who are you to judge another's servant" (v. 4)? Instead, we are to love them by giving up our own preferences if we think they would be confused by something we do. Maybe that is listening to certain music, dressing a certain way, or wearing certain makeup. Just because we have the right to do something doesn't make it right for us to do so if it offends or weakens someone else's faith.

Lord, thank You for the instruction in Your Word. Give us grace to lovingly encourage those You've accepted for the sake of Your great Name, amen.

If your brother is grieved . . . you are no longer walking in love. . . . Therefore let us pursue the things which make for peace and the things by which one may edify another.

Romans 14:15, 19

The plans of God bring ebb and flow—
His wisdom thus ordains it.
Prosperity to want may go,
As His good hands arrange it.
Both day and night dispense His grace;
Both work to serve His pleasure.
By day we know the glorious Face
At night we learn to treasure.

We err to think the darkness bad,
When shadows mask our knowing.
For there refreshing dew is had
That keeps the flowers growing.
The waxing and the waning moon
Both work to mark the season.
The winter dawn and dusk of June
Alike display His reason.

Shall we then seek that He explain
The circle of His blessing?
Our daily rhythms here maintain
Great patterns there expressing.
For sorrows come until the Day
When Night itself will vanish,
Till Wisdom has its perfect way,
And Light will Darkness banish.

The happy soul is then content
To know that He is faithful,
And through each difficult event
Remembers to be grateful.
For God commands each circumstance
To serve those of His calling.
His care enjoins the nightengale
To sing when dusk is falling.

So I will praise Him in the night,
This globe of sorrows surely turns.
See there His stars of promise bright;
Behold, the light of dawn returns.

Poem inspired by the June 1st entry of Morning and Evening: Daily Readings by Charles Haddon Spurgeon.

SO I WILL

Praise Him

IN THE NIGHT

*God called the light Day, and the darkness
He called Night. So the evening and the
morning were the first day.*

Genesis 1:5

Unquestionably the most famous galactic star cluster in the heavens, the Pleiades form a glittering group of what appears to the naked eye to be six to ten closely spaced stars. A pair of binoculars or a small telescope, however, reveals dozens more icy blue, diamond-like stars. The Pleiades have been revered by many different cultures since antiquity. To the Greeks, they were the Seven Sisters. To medieval German farmers, they were a hen and her chicks. And to the modern-day Japanese, they are known as the "Subaru" and are used as the very recognizable logo on their namesake brand of cars. The beauty of the Pleiades simply can't be ignored or overlooked.

The Lord desires Christians be just as noticeable and just as compelling. If we let the truth of the gospel shine through our priorities, motives, words, and deeds, we will be lights into the spiritual darkness around us. Through our humble witness, we can lead people to wonder about and explore what makes us shine with hope. What a privilege to be ambassadors for Christ and to share the amazing good news: "But now the righteousness of God has been manifested apart from the law, although the Law and the Prophets bear witness to it—the righteousness of God through faith in Jesus Christ for all who believe. For there is no distinction: for all have sinned and fall short of the glory of God, and are justified by his grace as a gift, through the redemption that is in Christ Jesus, whom God put forward as a propitiation by his blood, to be received by faith" (Romans 3:21–25 ESV). Now that's something that can't be ignored! What a great Savior! What a great salvation!

Those who are wise will shine
like the brightness of the heavens,
and those who lead many to righteousness,
like the stars for ever and ever.

Daniel 12:3 NIV

Wise
AND
Bright

Accounted with the hosts of heaven
Are saints our Lord commends as wise;
Proclaiming God's true righteousness,
They shine as light to darkened eyes.

Glimpsing God
IN THE ANDROMEDA GALAXY

Your power, scope, and splendor
I see in smallest part;
Yet when I see You clearer,
There's worship in my heart.

On clear autumn nights in the Northern Hemisphere, a tiny fuzzy spot can be seen with the naked eye in the constellation of Andromeda. With binoculars, the spot becomes a hazy, extended object in comparison to the pinpoint stars surrounding it. Larger telescopes and timed-exposure photographs reveal the true nature of this mysterious small cloud. It is in fact a gigantic spiral galaxy, so huge that even the unaided eye can see its core, though it is an amazing 2.5 million light-years away.

Discovered centuries earlier, this beautiful celestial object was documented as item #31 in an eighteenth-century catalog of faint objects kept by French astronomer Charles Messier. Hence it bears the name M31. Because of its size and relatively close proximity to our Milky Way Galaxy, it has figured prominently in the gradual realization by astronomers that the cosmos consists of "island universes." That is, astronomers have come to realize that galaxies are separated from one another by vast, largely empty spaces.

For many years—before telescopes were powerful enough to discern its individual stars—M31 was thought to be a giant gaseous nebula, embedded within the nearby stars. Even now, it is sometimes called the Great Andromeda Nebula. But research has revealed it to be a magnificent, distinct spiral galaxy comprised of over a trillion stars, with smaller neighboring galaxies and star clusters slowly circling its mysterious massive core.

When we see M31 and begin to grasp the vast, glorious, virtually unsearchable splendor of its nature, we are reminded of its even more glorious Maker. How dimly we glimpse His magnificence. How little we really understand of His majesty, power, and authority. May God open our eyes today to behold Him anew and our hearts to worship Him as never before. He is incomprehensibly powerful, unsearchably and magnificently intelligent, and gloriously beautiful. Unequalled in grace and wisdom, our Lord is also infinite in love.

Now to the King eternal, immortal,
invisible, to God who alone is wise, be
honor and glory forever and ever. Amen.

1 Timothy 1:17

What am *I* doing in the kingdom?
What am I *doing* in the kingdom?

───────── ❧ ─────────

In 1922, the International Astronomical Union sanctioned a list of eighty-eight constellations that are now regarded as the "official" set. Until that time, the names, patterns, and boundaries of the constellations varied from place to place, even as early maps of the New World varied from one explorer to the next. Among the stellar groups adopted into the list were two very unlikely choices: the constellations Microscopium and Telescopium. These were invented by the renowned French astronomer Nicolas Louis de Lacaille, who meticulously mapped nearly 10,000 stars in the Southern Hemisphere. Both constellations are squeezed into spaces between brighter, more recognizable ones. If they were viewable from the Northern Hemisphere, most suburbanites would find them too faint to actually see. Indeed, even if you could see them, they look nothing like the objects for which they're named. Lacaille, a moral and humble man of science, evidently included them to honor the contribution of these two new optical instruments—the microscope and the telescope—to the study of nature.

In 1 Timothy 1, the apostle Paul marvels at his inclusion in God's redemptive purpose. Keenly aware of his earlier blasphemy, persecution, and insolence (v. 13), he reckons himself in verse 15 as the "chief" of sinners. His humble gratitude is an excellent model for us. How is it that we, that is, I (of all people) should understand the need for a Savior and receive grace to repent and believe? What am *I* doing in the kingdom? Such contrite thinking will guide our conversations with others about Christ in a spirit of loving patience.

As members of God's kingdom, we should also be characterized by a desire for service. What are we *doing* in the kingdom? God has given us each a part to play. We are encouraged to "present yourselves to God as being alive from the dead, and your members to God as instruments of righteousness" (Romans 6:13). Just like optical instruments in the hands of a scientist, our lives and energies are to be "consecrated and useful to the master of the house, ready for any good work" (2 Timothy 2:21 RSV).

Lord Jesus, thank You for saving me. Use me as a willing instrument to make great Your marvelous Name, amen.

What Am I Doing in the Kingdom?

This is a faithful saying and worthy of all acceptance, that Christ Jesus came into the world to save sinners, of whom I am chief. However, for this reason I obtained mercy, that in me first Jesus Christ might show all longsuffering, as a pattern to those who are going to believe on Him for everlasting life.

1 Timothy 1:15–16

Spinning silently in beauty
Moves our special planet—
Much more than sea and granite.
Life is in its ev'ry crevasse,
Land and sea abounding—
So varied and astounding!
God, it was, who made it happen,
Author of its glory,
In Genesis, the story.

OUR Special EARTH

NASA

THERE IS A STRONG BIAS IN THE SCIENTIFIC COMMUNITY AGAINST THE IDEA THAT Earth is unique in any way or shows any evidence of a Designer. This belief actually has a name: the Copernican Principle. It is held as a fundamental tenet in many institutions of modern astronomy and astrobiology. It was the Polish astronomer Nicolaus Copernicus who theorized in the early sixteenth century that Earth and the other known planets circle the Sun, rather than the Sun orbiting Earth. The philosophical effect of his writings was to remove Earth from the center of the cosmos, a monumental switch from the teaching of the Roman Catholic Church at the time.

While there are aspects of the Copernican Principle that are commendable—caution in science is always good—the principle encourages its supporters to downplay or even ignore increasingly obvious facts about Earth and its life. In short, the odds of a world having by accident the combination of qualities that characterize Earth—and that are vital for sustaining life—are vanishingly small. For starters, a planet must exist in the "inhabitable zone" around its star. Not too close so that it would overheat and not too far away so that everything would freeze. The star must be a stable one. Many aren't. Some stars pulsate or emit highly lethal amounts of radiation—or even huge, intensely hot streamers of electrically charged gas. Many are in multiple star systems that over time disrupt the orbits of any planets in the system. Planets should not wobble, something kept in check by the presence of a large moon. And planets should have a magnetic field to protect them from charged particles, an atmosphere to protect them from cosmic rays, and an environment that contains certain specific molecules in the right quantities, and . . . the list goes on and on. The Lord made Earth to wonderfully satisfy every requirement for sustaining its diverse and abundant life. In Isaiah 6:3, the seraphim who worship God day and night from the magnificent vantage point of *heaven* are heard to pronounce a surprising perspective, worthy of our contemplation today: "The whole *earth* is full of His glory." Let us join the angels in worshiping Him for His creative genius, which flourishes everywhere in our most remarkable world.

For *thus says the* LORD,
Who created the heavens,
Who is God,
Who formed the earth and made it,
Who has established it,
Who did not create it in vain,
Who formed it to be inhabited:
"I am the LORD, and there is no other."

Isaiah 45:18

*"I am the Alpha and the Omega, the Beginning
and the End," says the Lord, "who is and who
was and who is to come, the Almighty."*

Revelation 1:8

As we set about our busy lives—whether it is at school, work, home, or ministry—let us take comfort in the fact that God knows everything that's going to happen to us as if it already did. God is not bound by time as we are. Neither is He bound by space. He is wondrously outside both, simultaneously knowing the smallest details of the tiniest molecules at opposite ends of His immeasurably grand universe. He views the past, present, and future all at once. Nothing escapes His attention. He's never surprised, and He never forgets. Everything is now to Him.

Though this is too marvelous to understand, it fills us with a reverent awe of Him. It can also bring us hope and peace. For as different as He is from us, He has pledged in a solemn covenant to love us forever—and in some strange sense, He's already there doing it!

Yes, the present world has many trials and difficulties, some quite severe. As the apostle Peter tells us in 1 Peter 1, these are meant to prove and deepen our faith, the precious gift that leads to our salvation. But he also reminds us that we live as aliens here; our true home awaits us in heaven with God Himself. He encourages us to "rest your hope fully upon the grace that is to be brought to you at the revelation of Jesus Christ (1 Peter 1:13). God is living in the good of that future moment right now. May we do so as well.

NASA, ESA, and the Hubble Heritage (STScI/AURA)-ESA/Hubble Collaboration. Acknowledgment: R. Chandar (University of Toledo) and J. Miller (University of Michigan)

Transcendence

Beyond the realm of eyes and ears,
The God of glory has no peers.
He sees in every age and place,
Transcendent over time and space.

THE FEAR OF THE LORD

Ten thousand times a thousand still—
The might of suns reduced to sand—
Thus so the vaunted sons of earth
Are brought to naught at His command.

Scores of globular star clusters orbit the center of our huge spiral galaxy, the Milky Way. Many are similar to this one, known as M80, which is located in the summer constellation Scorpio. Most contain hundreds of thousands of stars, though the largest may hold more than a million.

The scriptural analogy between the number of stars in the heavens and the number of grains of sand on the seashore is a well-chosen one. Our galaxy alone is thought to contain at least 200 billion stars! If this weren't hard enough to comprehend, astronomers now know there are billions of other galaxies stretching through space. God is frightfully powerful! Psalm 33:6 tells us that "by the word of the Lord the heavens were made, and all the host of them by the breath of His mouth." Each of the heavenly host—each twinkling star—is really an unimaginably colossal cauldron of churning and flaming plasma. Our small Sun alone could hold over a million Earths inside. That there could exist a Being who simply speaks such things into existence is truly a cause for wonder, humility, and fear.

The book of Proverbs was specifically written to teach us wisdom. Its most primary lesson is this: "The fear of the Lord is the beginning of knowledge" (1:7). We understand nothing until we first understand that we are creatures and that an almighty, uncompromising Being made us for His purposes. Jesus' followers asked Him the all-important question: "What must we do, to be doing the works of God?" His answer was timeless: "This is the work of God, that you believe in him whom he has sent." (John 6:28–29 ESV).

Do you believe that God sent His Son, Jesus, into the world to redeem us from sin? God didn't have to do this, but He graciously provided His own Son as a substitute for us. Christ took the punishment that should have been ours on the cross. What does God ask from us in return? Simply to turn and believe. "For God so loved the world, that he gave his only Son, that whoever believes in him should not perish but have eternal life" (John 3:16 ESV). Tell Jesus today that you believe He died for you, and pray that He will wash away your sins. Then praise the Son for His sacrifice.

Kiss the Son,
lest he be angry, and you perish in the way. . . .
Blessed are all who take refuge in him.

Psalm 2:12 ESV

He brings princes to naught and
reduces the rulers of this world to
nothing.

Isaiah 40:23 NIV

Beware
of Idols

Not to planets, stars, or Sun,
Nor to other idols run.
Christ belongs upon the throne;
Glory be to God alone.

S<small>EVERAL TIMES IN THE BOOK OF</small> D<small>EUTERONOMY, THE</small> L<small>ORD WARNS</small> Israel to avoid worshiping the heavenly hosts—a customary practice among the nations surrounding them. Great temples and extravagant ceremonies devoted to the deities of the Sun, Moon, and stars were common at that time. Lacking our present understanding of astronomy, it isn't hard to imagine how ancient cultures might be tempted to ascribe power or deity to them. The Sun and Moon are clearly linked to the times and seasons that govern agriculture and animal husbandry and, with them, material want and plenty. The bright planets move about the fixed constellations in odd patterns, which aren't discernable within a single lifetime. Hence they too seem to have special power or authority which even the stars do not. Planetary groupings that coincided with great losses or victories would have been notable occurrences. Without our modern city lights to dim them, the stars and planets were undoubtedly much more noticed, regarded, and considered than at present.

The larger issue the Lord called Israel (and now us) to consider, however, is to whom or what do we give our attention, affection, time, and money. In other words, who or what do we worship? It's not only in the pseudoscience of astrology that people today invest time and effort to find happiness. Countless material pleasures keep us from knowing, loving, and trusting God. Are you drawn away from God by anything in your life? If so, put Christ back upon the throne of your heart, where He rightfully belongs. "For all the gods of the peoples are idols, but the L<small>ORD</small> made the heavens" (1 Chronicles 16:26).

And beware lest you raise your eyes to heaven, and when you see the sun and the moon and the stars, all the host of heaven, you be drawn away and bow down to them and serve them, things that the L<small>ORD</small> your God has allotted to all the peoples under the whole heaven.

Deuteronomy 4:19 <small>ESV</small>

The God of the Bible is revealed as a God who loves to name things. Day, night, Earth, seas, Adam, Israel . . . these are all names the Lord chose for His creations. Jesus also seems to have enjoyed special nicknames for His friends. Cephas He called Peter, the Rock. Thomas was Didymus, the Twin. And He nicknamed the brothers James and John the "Sons of Thunder," evidently a comment on the personality of their father, Zebedee.

Similarly, astronomical objects take on various names as they are cataloged formally and informally. This beautiful image shows the star cluster known as Hodge 301, a grouping found within the nebula alternatively known as 30 Doradus, the Tarantula Nebula and NGC 2070. The name 30 Doradus indicates that this system is found in the southern constellation of Dorado the Swordfish. The designation "NGC" identifies this entity as a member of the formal New General Catalog of faint nonstellar objects. The more informal name "Tarantula Nebula" arose from the region's general appearance in small telescopes or binoculars. Personal listings can also become widely accepted in astronomy, such as the Charles Messier Catalog or the list by Paul Hodge that includes this cluster.

God has names for all the stars, as impossible as that seems. Jesus further informs us that God numbers every hair on our heads (Matthew 10:30). Though impossible for us, these things are not difficult for Him, as He is infinitely almighty. The number of people on Earth—a vast number to us—is a paltry one for Him. Do you suppose that He who named all the glorious stars also has a special name for you? Why don't you ask Him?

He counts the number of the stars;
He calls them all by name.
Great is our Lord, and mighty in power;
His understanding is infinite.

Psalm 147:4–5

What Name
Has He *for Me?*

He named the demarcation of
His radiance "Day" from "Night";
He called twin Thomas "Ditymus,"
And Jacob, "Israelite."
He leads each of His starry host
from anonymity.
Oh, ask the "Sons of Thunder" this:
What name has He for me?

*The end of all things is at hand; therefore be
self-controlled and sober-minded.*

1 Peter 4:7 ESV

IN 1877, ITALIAN ASTRONOMER GIOVANNI SCHIAPARELLI SAW SOME unusual straight-line features on the planet Mars that he called *canali*, which translated into English as "channels" or "canals." Other astronomers around the world also reported seeing them—notably Percival Lowell, founder of the Lowell Observatory in Flagstaff, Arizona, where some years later Pluto was discovered. Lowell was convinced that the canals were of unnatural origin and championed the idea that an intelligent race installed them as a large irrigation project to route water from Mars's polar caps to the dry equatorial region of the planet. After all, in like manner, engineers on Earth were busily involved in making the Suez and Panama canals to increase prosperity on our home planet. Mars was also similar to Earth, with days of comparable length, polar caps, and seasons.

Other scientists disagreed, calculating that the atmospheric pressure on Mars was too low to permit liquid water on its surface and that the prevailing temperature was much too low to easily support life. Yet another group disagreed because they simply couldn't see the canals, even with larger and better telescopes. Unfortunately for them all, celestial photography was in its infancy, so photographs did not bring any clarity to the issue.

Meanwhile, Lowell spent many years detailing the canals in catalogs, identifying oases and assigning them all names. It wasn't until the *Mariner 4* spacecraft flew by Mars in 1965 that the issue was settled: there were no canals. Apparently, what Schiaparelli, Lowell, and others saw were optical illusions: small lines that our brain creates to link and organize a visual field of patchy spots.

What we learn from this is that scientists make mistakes and data gets misinterpreted. As believers, we should be joyful in spirit, sober in our thinking, and careful in our judgments. This applies to interpreting Scripture as well as nature. There is a natural tendency in us all to see what we want to see rather than what's really there.

Lord, help us to think through the scientific, doctrinal, and moral issues of our day with clarity and honesty in a way that honors You and reveals truth, amen.

*"Do not judge by appearances, but
judge with right judgment."*

John 7:24 ESV

Clear
Thinking

Care adorns the souls whose goal is pleasing God,
For sober minds are given to His ways.
Wise as serpents, yet as innocent as doves,
Clear thinking brings them straightway through the maze.

I am a sojourner on the earth;
hide not your commandments from me!

Psalm 119:19 ESV

Of the eighty-eight official constellations, at least fifteen have to do with the sea, sailing, or sea life. It's little wonder. Where better to contemplate the stars than from the deck of a ship, drifting on the ocean under the clear, dark skies? Good sailors are keen observers too; constantly on the lookout for dangers from winds, waves, and rocks.

To ancient seafaring cultures, the stars would have been at once both mysterious and comforting. The patterns of the constellations would have been very familiar to them. Their order and positions predictable and helpful as signals of the changing seasons. Then, too, there is ample time for thought while sailing across the great seas. Time to consider, dream, and pray. Time to assess what's really important, what relationships matter most, and what things really satisfy. May God help us evaluate our journey through life rightly. For in the end, our true home is not here, but with Him in heaven.

Nevertheless I am continually with You;
You hold me by my right hand.
You will guide me with Your counsel,
And afterward receive me to glory.
Whom have I in heaven but You?
And there is none upon earth that I desire besides You.
My flesh and my heart fail;
But God is the strength of my heart and my portion forever.

Psalm 73:23–26

HARBOR OF MY
Heart's Desire

Harbor of my heart's desire,
Lord, in Thee I seek my rest.
Thou my anxious thoughts retire;
Pressing cares, Thy grace divests.
Oh, to hear Your voice so tender—
Clear and gentle as the dove!
Call me into quiet waters;
Still my anchor in Thy love.

Harbor of my heart's desire,
All my longings meet in Thee.
Let the joys of earth conspire—
They no satisfactions be.
Earnest as the watchman searching,
Restless here my soul does roam.
Guide me by Thy present blessing
Into my eternal home.

DO NOT
Be a *Wanderer*

Do not be like the wanderer,
Who has no fixed abode.
Together, grouped with other saints,
Let not your gleam erode.
Instead, as lights, go form a group
The lost will recognize:
A constellation marked by love
Seen bright beneath the skies.

ESO

And let us consider how to stir up one another to love and good works,
not neglecting to meet together, as is the habit of some, but encouraging
one another, and all the more as you see the Day drawing near.

Hebrews 10:24–25 ESV

COALS STAY HOTTER AND BRIGHTER WHEN CLUSTERED TOGETHER. BUT separate one from the group, and it quickly grows cold and faint. So it is with Christians. The apostle Peter suggests that God designed us to operate together as living stones collected to form a spiritual temple (1 Peter 2:5). Similarly, the apostle Paul encourages us to act like the human body: many individual parts, each with their own function, working together to accomplish the dictates and desires of the Head, who is Christ (1 Corinthians 12:12–31). We obviously can't do this alone. We weren't meant to.

Just as obvious, the patterns we call constellations would make no recognizable pattern at all if the stars in them moved about from night to night. The stars of the constellations are not members of a physical cluster, but rather they form an optical grouping along our line of sight—some relatively nearby and others farther away. But they all lie at such immense distances that their motions can be discerned only over hundreds of years. Very slowly and barely noticeable, they change their constellations' shapes. The only "stars" that wander are the planets. In fact, the word *planet* means "wanderer." Because they are tens of thousands of times closer than the nearest stars, their motions, though slow at times, are generally noticeable against the background stars, even from night to night. The planets, of course, are very different from stars, though they resemble them to the naked eye. Planets shine by reflected light, not light produced within.

Jude warns us against spiritual wanderers—those who drift into church and may look like others but have no real spiritual life inside. They are recognizably selfish. But may it not be so with us! Collected together with others, each on individual paths, may we form a glorious grouping whose selfless love provokes the notice and interest of everyone around us.

These are spots in your love feasts, while they feast
with you without fear, serving only themselves. They
are clouds without water . . . wandering stars for
whom is reserved the blackness of darkness forever.

Jude 1:12–13

But Jesus answered them, "You are wrong, because you know
neither the Scriptures nor the power of God."

Matthew 22:29 ESV

Sɪᴛ ᴘᴇʀꜰᴇᴄᴛʟʏ sᴛɪʟʟ ꜰᴏʀ ᴀ ᴍᴏᴍᴇɴᴛ. Dᴏ ʏᴏᴜ ꜰᴇᴇʟ ᴅɪᴢᴢʏ? Dᴏ ʏᴏᴜ sᴇɴsᴇ the wind blowing through your hair? No, probably not, but maybe you should. Do you realize that at this very second you're spinning four times faster than a tornado and moving across the galaxy at more than two hundred times the speed of an M16 bullet? Remarkably, it's true. Despite our inability to sense it, the expanse of space is so large and the gravitational force of the Sun and galaxy's center so strong that we move at these truly astronomical speeds to satisfy our "normal" orbital motions.

Here's how the numbers work. Compared to other celestial bodies, Earth is tiny yet it is nearly 25,000 miles in circumference! It takes twenty-four hours to turn once on its axis—that means we're moving at more than 1,000 miles per hour, much faster than the 250 mile-per-hour tornado. Likewise, Earth completes its colossal orbit around the Sun (584 million miles) in just 365 days, but it must move at a speed of around 67,000 miles per hour to do so. And even more astounding, our entire solar system is being flung around the center of our gigantic spiral galaxy at just under 500,000 miles per hour—much faster than the M16's bullet.

There is a life-changing lesson to be learned here. If we cannot readily sense amazingly true physical realities, why do we doubt the equally true (and even more amazing) spiritual realities? We can't *feel* God, but He exists. We can't *sense* that He's holding the universe together "by the word of His power" (Hebrews 1:3 ESV), but He is. We don't see angels or demons, but Jesus spoke plainly of both. We can't even tell our own spiritual state before God unless the Spirit opens the eyes of our understanding to see.

Today, let us humble ourselves before God and His truthful Word. It says He is faithful, loving, and wise, and He is—whether our feelings confirm it or not. It says He is our Help and our Shield, and we can surely trust that He will be today, tomorrow, and forever. It says He works all things together for the good of those who love Him—and we can trust Him to do just that.

"If I have told you earthly things
and you do not believe, how can you
believe if I tell you heavenly things?"

John 3:12 ESV

Sensing
the Truth

If stars could speak and tell us of their view
Of grand celestial movements, tracks and speeds,
We'd be the better counseled to see through
The fog that from our feelings e'er proceeds.
Thus so, should angels tell us all they see
Of God's transcendent means for guiding men,
Our hearts, so blind, would surely better be
Informed with truth to trust His Word again.

PRAISE HIM
Completely

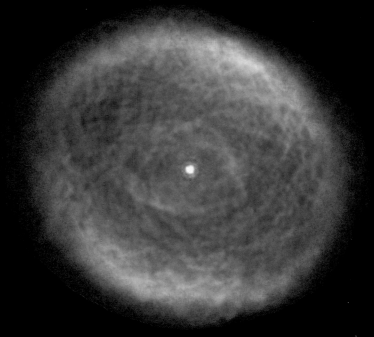

Praise Him in the Arts
For the Sciences . . .
Praise Him in the Sciences . . .
For His Art.

I HIS AMAZING AND BEAUTIFUL OBJECT IS FOUND IN THE
constellation of Lepus the Hare, hiding in the winter sky
beneath the feet of Orion the Hunter. Cataloged by astronomers as IC 418, this object is known as a *planetary nebula*
because, in small telescopes, its circular shape appears very
much like the disk of a planet. In reality, the shape is caused by
layers of gas that have been ejected from the central star due to
complex physical processes there. As one shell of gas moves
away, cools, and slows down, it is then flooded by ultraviolet
radiation from the star, which causes it to fluoresce. The colors
represent the various chemical constituents (nitrogen, hydrogen, and oxygen) of the shells. The remarkable patterns within
this and other planetaries are assumed to be based at least in
part on the rotation of their central stars, but they remain
poorly understood.

Look around you—there's no greater scientist or artist than
God Himself. Therefore, the artistic sensibilities of men and
women should rightly be employed in honoring God for the
exquisite engineering and mathematical foundations of His
universe. Likewise, those with scientific and engineering skill
should humbly engage in worshiping God for the artistic
beauty and intricate simplicity of His creative genius. The left
lobe of our brains is where logical and sequential thinking—
like an engineer's—is seated. The right lobe supports more
intuitive, holistic thinking—like an artist's. Let us purpose
today to use our whole brain—all that He's given us—to
explore, comprehend, imitate, and celebrate His universe and
then to return manifold praise to God.

Who is like You, O LORD, among the gods?
Who is like You, glorious in holiness,
Fearful in praises, doing wonders?

Pursue
Four Things

May God's Word help aim us right,
Balanced like a crosshair's site.
Then we'll find four things increase:
Righteousness, faith, love, and peace.

———————— ⚜ ————————

NASA, ESA, STScI and STScI

On summer nights under dark skies, one can see overhead the beautiful glowing band of the Milky Way. It shimmers with the combined light of millions upon millions of distant stars that are grouped together in a colossal, flattened, slowly spiraling structure that's too big to visually grasp—our galaxy. Astronomers now understand that the Sun and its planets are located inside the galaxy, positioned in a spiral arm about halfway out from the center to one edge. When we look up on summer nights, we're looking along the pinwheel. And as we aim our gaze in the direction of Sagittarius, we are looking toward the galaxy's center. Sagittarius is taking aim himself. In Greek mythology, the constellation is said to depict a Centaur (half horse, half man) holding a bow and shooting toward the bright star Antares, the heart of Scorpio, the scorpion. Another celestial arrow is found nearby: the tiny constellation of Sagitta the Arrow—on the opposite side of Sagittarius from the scorpion that he's pursuing.

In 2 Timothy 2:22, we are told to "take aim at," or "pursue," four divinely inspired things: righteousness, faith, love, and peace. By pursuing righteousness—that is, right living—we imitate Him who is Righteousness itself. Doing what's right without faith, however, is not pleasing to Him, as we read in Hebrews 11:7 and Romans 14:23. Doing right—with faith that moves mountains—but without love, leaves us with nothing (1 Corinthians 13). But doing what's right, in faith and with love, can be so hard that sometimes we act anxiously (or joylessly), so the Scripture encourages us to pursue peace as well. What an amazingly balanced list!

Lord, we thank You for the beautiful heavens, where we can learn of Your glory. Thank You as well for Your inspired Word that so accurately and lovingly guides us to live fruitful lives. Help us to simultaneously pursue righteousness, faith, love, and peace for the honor of Your name. And keep our souls pointed in the direction that marks the center of Your perfect will, amen.

But in a great house there are not only vessels of gold and silver, but also of wood and clay, some for honor and some for dishonor. Therefore if anyone cleanses himself from the latter, he will be a vessel for honor, sanctified and useful for the Master, prepared for every good work. Flee also youthful lusts; but pursue righteousness, faith, love, peace with those who call on the Lord out of a pure heart.

2 Timothy 2:20–22

THE WORD *HOLY* IN THE BIBLE COMMUNICATES THE IDEA OF BEING "separate" or "consecrated." As sons and daughters of God, we are called to be holy like our Father: separate from evil and fully consecrated to righteousness. But as the word *holy* relates to God, it carries the deeper meaning of being totally unlike everything else, separate in His very essence from the created order. This quality produces in Him a purity of being that defies description.

In Isaiah chapter 6, we are told of the glorious seraphim: fantastic creatures who perpetually fly around the throne of God declaring His glory with voices that make even the doorposts of heaven shake. They each have six wings: two to cover their faces, two to cover their feet, and two to fly. Evidently, beholding God, the uncreated One, is completely overwhelming—even to angelic beings. What they are heard to cry out is "Holy, holy, holy, is the LORD of hosts; the whole earth is full of His glory!" (v. 3). Scholars tell us that the repetition of a phrase or word in the Hebrew language is a way of emphasizing it. Likewise, various theologians have pointed out that this is the only quality of God ever repeated three times in a row. God is never, for instance, called "Faithful, faithful, faithful" or "Love, love, love," though He clearly is these things. It is His holiness or "otherness" that Scripture itself emphasizes. The name God revealed to Moses for Himself at the burning bush captures His stark and incomprehensible separateness: "I AM WHO I AM" (Exodus 3:14). We are told in Job that even the stars are not pure in His eyes (25:5). Imagine looking directly at the Sun! The Moon is 93 million miles from the Sun. It reflects its light to Earth with an efficiency of only 12 percent (similar to a piece of burnt charcoal); yet the full Moon lights up the entire night sky! Among the other stars, there are some known to be even 20,000 times more luminous than the Sun! But the brightest of the stars are nothing compared to the dazzlingly bright holiness of their Creator.

Oh Lord, You are holy. Who can comprehend Your purity, power, and intrinsic righteousness? Receive today from us the glory You are due. Hallowed be Your name!

The lamp of the body is the eye. If therefore your eye is good, your whole body will be full of light.

Matthew 6:22

GOD'S
Holiness

Oh, how much purer than the light of midnight's moon,
Or keener white than shining stars, or Sun at noon.
Are His amazing eyes, that take us to His soul—
The seat of holiness—which seraphs e'er extol.

Behold, even the moon is not bright
and the stars are not pure in His eyes.

Job 25:5 ESV

Astronomical *Mercy*

*No eye has seen, nor ear has heard
The fullness found within Your Word
Of endless mercy, love, and grace
That's higher still than outer space.
Oh, Lord, I kneel before You now
And humbly ask that You'd allow
My soul to touch this endless love
That permeates to realms above.*

K<small>INDNESS IS A VIRTUE THAT CARRIES A LONG WAY</small>. P<small>EOPLE WHO ARE FULL OF</small> goodness, mercy, and kindness toward us are the ones we like to be around. In the Old Testament Hebrew language, the word *checed* (pronounced kheh'-sed) means all these things. It is a word derived from a root word that carries the idea of "ardor" or "zeal" to bless. Our English Bibles translate the word *checed* using various words like "kindness," "lovingkindness," and "goodness." But chief among words used for it is "mercy."

In Psalm 57:10, we read that God's mercy "reaches unto the heavens." Consider this: perhaps you have a shopping mall or grocery store that's four miles from your home. When was the last time you told someone it was 6,437,376 millimeters away? "That's ridiculous," you say, and you'd be right. Millimeters are much too small to measure a distance of miles. In like manner, miles are much too small a measure to relate a distance that reaches to the heavens. The nearest star is four light-years away, which is nearly 24 trillion miles. But the most distant stars in our galaxy are more than15,000 times farther away than that and the stars in the farthest galaxies, billions of times farther still. Psalm 103:11 makes it plain: "For as high as the heavens are above the earth, so great is his steadfast love [*checed*] toward those who fear him" (ESV). That is amazing, but it's not the end. Psalm 36:5 tells us that God's mercy not only extends to the heavens but is in the heavens. In Psalm 108:4, God tells us that His mercy is great above the heavens. Do you get the point? It's hard to imagine how the Lord could more plainly tell us that He is *unimaginably* full of mercy, that there exists in Him an inextinguishable ardor to bless. What are your burdens today? Health? Relationships? Finances? Barrenness? Go to God. As Psalm 136 repeats over and over and over: "His [*checed*] endures forever."

*Oh, give thanks to the L*ORD*, for He is good!*

For His mercy endures forever.

Oh, give thanks to the God of gods!

For His mercy endures forever.

Oh, give thanks to the Lord of lords!

For His mercy endures forever:

To Him who alone does great wonders,

For His mercy endures forever;

To Him who by wisdom made the heavens,

For His mercy endures forever.

Psalm 136:1–5

God's Tadpoles

Oh, what grand celestial might
The Tadpole sweeps across the night!
Yet this cosmic truth still stands:
The Tadpole swims within His hands.

OTHERWISE KNOWN BY THE LACKLUSTER NAME UGC 10214, THIS spectacular celestial object, dubbed the "Tadpole Galaxy," was one of the first to be imaged by the Advanced Camera for Surveys—an instrument installed by astronauts into the Hubble Space Telescope in the spring of 2002. The "tail" of the Tadpole is evidently gas, stars, and dust pulled away from the body of the galaxy by the gravitational interaction of another galaxy nearby. Computer simulations of such encounters have shown that complex arcs and distorted galactic shapes are to be expected. But the sweeping scale of this stellar system boggles the mind; the tail is estimated to be 280,000 light-years long. With a single light-year equaling about 6 trillion miles, this makes the length of the tail 168 million trillion miles! As astounding as this is, even more remarkable than the "tail" is the large number of background galaxies that appear in this one image—more than 6,000! Most of these galaxies are tens of thousands of light-years across and are obviously separated by even more colossal distances. Incredible as it may seem, this picture shows an area of the sky no bigger than the size of Lincoln's eye on a penny held at arm's length! Imagine then how many galactic systems are in the universe! Astronomers believe there are more than 100 billion!

In Isaiah 40, we're told that God can scoop out the waters of the oceans with His palm and that He can mark off the heavens with the span of His hand. As vast as the Tadpole Galaxy is to us, to Him it is truly only like a tiny squirming tadpole within His hands. Let us bow before the Lord as the singularly powerful, forever incomparable, awesome, majestic, and eternal God.

To whom will you liken Me, and make Me equal
And compare Me, that we should be alike?

Isaiah 46:5

In Psalm 48, we're invited by the sons of Korah to consider the greatness of God by touring, so to speak, the grand city of Jerusalem. Consider the power and faithfulness of God that enabled its construction there atop Mount Zion. Think of its beauty, its majesty, its remarkable size, its seemingly endless towers, bulwarks, and palaces. Think of the safety found there, the worship in the temple, the righteous judgments of the King. These things so remarkably spoke of the Lord and His presence that the psalmists could say metaphorically: "This is God" (v. 14).

A similar experience of wonder and awe in God fills us as we gaze into the heavens. In this image of what has been called the "Mystic Mountain" (a portion of the Carina Nebula), we marvel at pillars of gas and dust light-years tall that roil and churn under the influence of many embedded, gas-jetting stars. Even the radiation from these stars is so great that it pushes and sculpts the nebula around them. There is power here, majesty, beauty, mystery, and grandeur. Consider today the heavens, and worship the incomparably great God who made them. He is our King and Guide—both in this life and forever.

> Great is the LORD, and greatly to be praised
> In the city of our God,
> In His holy mountain.
> Beautiful in elevation,
> The joy of the whole earth,
> Is Mount Zion on the sides of the north,
> The city of the great King.
> God is in her palaces;
> He is known as her refuge. . . .
> Walk about Zion,
> And go all around her.
> Count her towers;
> Mark well her bulwarks;
> Consider her palaces;
> That you may tell it to the generation following.
> For this is God,
> Our God forever and ever;
> He will be our guide
> Even to death.
>
> Psalm 48:1–3, 12–14

Taken from NKJV. Used by permission. Copyright © 1982 by Thomas Nelson, Inc. and the Holman 70th Anniversary Team (NKJV)

THIS IS *God*

Spire after spire,
In mystery and might;
These declare God's glory
Like cities in the night.
O Lord, receive my worship;
My joy is that You be,
As Guardian of Your splendors,
My Guide eternally.

STARS ARE NOT ALL THE SAME. THEY VARY NOT ONLY IN BRIGHTNESS, BUT also in size and color. Their colors disclose their temperatures—in the same way a heated iron bar in the blacksmith's fire reveals its temperature. Glowing first a dull red, it grows hotter through a yellow phase and then eventually becomes blue or white-hot. Stellar temperatures are similar. The cooler stars are red; the hot ones are blue or white. Younger stars are hotter, and they generally cool with age. These hotter stars are more luminous than cooler ones, so if they're the same size, they can be seen farther away.

The winter star Electra, located within the bright cluster known as the Seven Sisters (the Pleiades), is a good example of a bright, blue-white young star. But large stars, even if they're cooler, can also be very luminous. The bright summer star Antares in Scorpio is such a star. It is a red supergiant, eight hundred times the diameter of the Sun and visually 10,000 times more luminous. It is one of the brighter stars in the sky, glowing intensely and seen splendidly more than six hundred light-years away.

We are called to be lights in the world. Each of us is given a measure of faith and gifts from the Lord to use in His service for the good of others. Some, like the servants in the parable of Matthew 25, have one (non-monetary) talent; others more. Some talents are less visible than others but are no less important. In all cases, we're rewarded by the Master for using and developing our gifts. Today let us consider how bright our lives shine. Older, "cooler" saints need be no fainter than younger, spiritually "hot" ones. Decide to shine brightly, whatever your state.

Lord Jesus, come stoke the fires of passion in our souls for You and Your kingdom. Help us shine brightly, guiding all to You and Your gospel for the glory of Your Name, amen.

> *There are also celestial bodies and terrestrial bodies; but the glory of the celestial is one, and the glory of the terrestrial is another. There is one glory of the sun, another glory of the moon, and another glory of the stars; for one star differs from another star in glory.*
>
> 1 Corinthians 15:40–41

DIFFERING
LIKE STARS

Electra is both hot and white,
A neighbor to the Sun.
Antares is a brighter light,
More distant, and not young.
No matter what our age or gifts,
Lord, may our service be
Bright as the star, whose glory lifts
Your fame for all to see.

FOR I BELIEVE
THE *Gospel*

How can I deny it,
But, oh, how can it be?
The mighty Lord of heaven
Is living now in me!
I cannot comprehend it,
And yet I know it's true;
For I believe the gospel,
And everything is new!

What life is this inside of me
That never was before?
What's welling up, compelling me
To worship and adore?
What Spirit moves and quickens now
To listen and obey?
What faithful sense directs somehow
When I don't get my way?

What interest builds inside of me
When now His Word is read?
What prompts me into charity
Where feelings once were dead?
What moves me forth to fellowship,
To share my sins and pride?
What conquers fear and faithlessness,
Producing peace inside?

How can I deny it,
But, oh, how can this be?
The One who made the heavens
Is living now in me!
I cannot comprehend it,
Yet wonderfully it's true;
For I believe the gospel,
And everything is new!

Therefore, if anyone is in Christ, he is a
new creation. The old has passed away;
behold, the new has come.

2 Corinthians 5:17 ESV

NEW STARS ARE SOMETHING OF A MIRACLE. THEY obviously begin somehow, but the precise conditions that trigger the collapse of large interstellar molecular clouds to form them are poorly understood. Many young star clusters are found in the density waves that give shape to the arms of spiral galaxies, or in regions where two interacting galaxies produce colossal gravitational tides. Somehow it would appear that these forces assist the process, but it isn't obvious why they should.

While the Christian's faith in God is eminently reasonable, the details surrounding the new birth of a soul are as mysterious and marvelous as the birth of a new star. Think of the apostle Paul—devoutly pursuing what he thought was right—but changed virtually overnight to hate what he previously valued. Many times, the Lord uses the stresses of life to draw souls to Himself. Still, the internal revelation that convinces a soul that the gospel is true and produces the faith to repent and believe is a wonderful gift that we should never take for granted.

For by grace you have been saved
through faith, and that not of your-
selves; it is the gift of God, not of works,
lest anyone should boast.

Ephesians 2:8–9

CERTAIN ACCOUNTING TASKS ARE BEST LEFT UNDONE. FOR INSTANCE, TABULATING the number of water molecules in the oceans, or numbering the grains of sand on their beaches, are senseless (and virtually impossible) tasks. The same is true for measuring the height of the heavens. The fastest known thing in our universe is the speed of light—186,282 miles per *second*. At this unfathomable speed, it takes light 5½ hours to reach distant Pluto, four years to reach the nearest star, 100,000 years to cross the Milky Way, 2½ million years to reach the nearest large galaxy like ours, and many billions of years to reach the faintest galaxies that telescopes can see. Light travels nearly 6 *trillion* miles in one year alone. Thus, it literally *would* be easier to count the grains of sand than to count the number of miles to the farthest reaches of the known universe.

In Isaiah 55:9, the Lord uses the height of the heavens to illustrate the incomparable difference between His ways and thoughts and our ways and thoughts. To say this is humbling is perhaps the greatest understatement ever uttered. He is our Creator; we are but creatures. By His great might and authority, He simply spoke the universe into existence. He spoke and it was! This alone shows that His ways *are* immeasurably higher than ours. His thoughts, too, are higher and deeper and wider than ours could ever be. But don't miss the exceedingly precious context of this verse: in unimaginable, unfathomable love, the Lord invites the world to turn to Him for mercy (v. 7).

Have you ever committed a sin that haunts you as unforgivable? Listen to what the Lord says: you may consider it unforgivable, but He doesn't. His thoughts are not like ours, and His love is infinitely higher. In another of His infinitely high ways, He's placed the perfect righteousness of Christ into our accounts so that He can extend pardon to us as Christians for even the most heinous sins. Listen again to God's appeal at the beginning of Isaiah 55, and be changed forever: "Ho! Everyone who thirsts, come to the waters; and you who have no money, come, buy and eat. . . . Listen carefully to Me, and eat what is good, and let your soul delight itself in abundance. Incline your ear, and come to Me. Hear, and your soul shall live" (vv. 1–3).

> *Let the wicked forsake his way,*
> *And the unrighteous man his thoughts;*
> *Let him return to the* LORD,
> *And He will have mercy on him;*
> *And to our God,*
> *For He will abundantly pardon.*
> *"For My thoughts are not your thoughts,*
> *Nor are your ways My ways," says the* LORD.
> *"For as the heavens are higher than the earth,*
> *So are My ways higher than your ways,*
> *And My thoughts than your thoughts."*
>
> Isaiah 55:7–9

Higher

THAN YOUR

THOUGHTS

How, I ask, oh how? How. can this be?
If it were not for telescopes that truly see
These things so grand and distant, I would have to say:
'Tis folly to believe the universe could be this way.
And yet astounding more is Love so deep and great
It flung the galaxies this far as to create
A means, a way to illustrate to men His grace;
To know His call to life, His fellowship, and His embrace.

Great are the works of the LORD,
studied by all who delight in them.

Psalm 111:2 ESV

What Do
You Study?

Should stomachs fill with candy
When there is more to eat?
Should souls delight in trifles
And not with heaven's meat?
Lord, cut the briars that choke us,
The lure of worldly things;
May our delight be knowing
The Love that study brings.

> *Therefore we must pay much closer attention to what*
> *we have heard, lest we drift away from it.*

Hebrews 2:1 ESV

THERE ARE A THOUSAND WAYS TO SPEND OUR TIME. THESE DAYS, WITH the convenience and extraordinary reach of the Internet, hours can evaporate while Web shopping, catching the news, or trying to stay in touch with others on our favorite social networking sites. There are myriad entertainment venues that call to us as well: movies, Web videos, video games, television shows, music, sports, arcades, and on and on. We're so inundated with entertainment options that most of us probably don't even know how many channels are on our televisions! While all these things have their place, God has given us far richer fare to engage our minds and spirits. Ultimately, our souls find their deepest satisfaction in knowing Him and relating to Him. But like every other activity, this takes pursuit and practice. It involves a commitment to study both the Lord and His works. We can find these both in His Word, but we can also learn much of Him by studying His works in nature.

And how much there is to study! Scientists could spend whole careers probing the intricacies of even one blade of grass. But nowhere are God's amazing knowledge, creativity, and power more loudly proclaimed than in the heavens. Take, for instance, the beautiful and wondrous Eskimo Nebula pictured here. In small telescopes, it looks vaguely like a face surrounded by a fur hood, but clearer views reveal strangely shaped bubbles and filaments of high-velocity gases—emitted in some yet unknown sequence by the troubled central star. What delight there is in probing and exploring such things! Each and every object in the heavens is fantastic in so many astounding ways.

In much the same way, what delight there is in probing and exploring God's mighty work of salvation. What mercy, love, faithfulness, grace, justice, righteousness, and peace are revealed at the Cross! It is surely to our detriment, as well as our family's, to drift away from looking into and loving these things more deeply.

Oh, Lord God, keep us from lives so caught up in worldly things that we stray away from meditating, studying, and delighting in You and Your great works, amen.

> *Of old you laid the foundation of the earth,*
> *and the heavens are the work of your hands.*

Psalm 102:25 ESV

And he was transfigured before them, and his face shone like the sun.

Matthew 17:2 ESV

JESUS. NAME ABOVE ALL NAMES. THE SUM AND CENTER OF ALL things. Heaven's highest Praise; mankind's finest Hope. His excellencies shame our loftiest estimations and grandest thoughts. Even angelic seraphs cover their bodies and faces with their wings as they fly near Him declaring, "Holy, holy, holy, is the Lord God Almighty" (Revelation 4:8 ESV). At a glimpse of Him, Isaiah said, "Woe is me! For I am lost" (Isaiah 6:5 ESV). Moses desired to see the Lord but was only permitted to look briefly at His back, for the Lord told him: "You cannot see my face, for man shall not see me and live" (Exodus 33:20 ESV). Even much later, the Israelites would hide from Moses until he made a veil to cover his face because "behold, the skin of his face shone and they were afraid to come near him" (Exodus 34:30 ESV). The apostle John was given a vision of heaven and wrote: "When I saw him, I fell at his feet as though dead" (Revelation 1:17 ESV). This is what he described: "His eyes were like a flame of fire, his feet were like burnished bronze, refined in a furnace. . . And his face was like the sun shining in full strength" (vv. 14–16 ESV).

The Sun is 109 times the diameter of Earth, making its volume able to hold 1,300,000 Earths. Its surface temperature is around 10,000 degrees Fahrenheit, and its core is 27 million degrees. Its energy source is nuclear fusion, which converts about 400 million tons of hydrogen into energy every second. The strength of the Sun, its energy output, is 500 billion-trillion horsepower. While these numbers are beyond comprehension, the glory of God exceeds them all. His face defies any created likeness.

Let today be a day of worship. God is unspeakably glorious, incomprehensibly powerful, and unfathomably holy, yet He calls us into relationship with Him. Jesus is Lord, and He's coming back. May our lives reflect these realities.

Again the high priest asked him, "Are you the Christ, the Son of the Blessed?" And Jesus said, "I am, and you will see the Son of Man seated at the right hand of Power, and coming with the clouds of heaven."

Mark 14:61–62 ESV

BEHOLD,
THE *SON OF*
GLORY COMES

Behold, the Son of Glory comes,
His face resplendent as the day,
From east to west great heralds cry:
"The former times have passed away."
He stands before adoring hosts;
Attendant beings voice acclaim:
"The Christ of God returns to Earth;
Bend down your knee, and bless His name."

LOCATED AT THE FOOT OF THE NORTHERN CROSS (OR ALTERNATIVELY, at the head of Cygnus the Swan) is arguably the most beautiful star in the summer sky. Its name is Albireo. Even with a small telescope, it can be resolved into a striking two-color double star. Its amber and azure components dazzle like gems amidst the scores of fainter white Milky Way stars seen around it. The larger star of the two is yellow and is itself a double star, though incapable of being seen as such except by large telescopes under ideal conditions. The smaller star is blue-green—a hot, fast-rotating star. The pair is located approximately 380 light-years away. Interestingly, the name Albireo is a misprint of an Arabic term that was from a Latin root, which itself was a mistranslation of another Arabic term derived from a Greek word!

The beautiful star Albireo reminds us of the amazing and even more mysteriously beautiful juxtaposition of wrath and mercy found at the foot of the cross. Here Love Incarnate, the God-man, Jesus Christ, met the righteous demands of God's justice. As our substitute, He paid with His life to secure forgiveness of our sins. God did both the condemning and redeeming. He both exacted punishment and paid for it at the same time. He poured out His furious wrath; yet in truly amazing grace, He saved man from experiencing it by taking it Himself. As Romans 3:26 puts it, He is both "just and the justifier of the one who has faith in Jesus."

O Lord, who can fathom Your glorious intentions and works? As the heavens declare Your glory, so Your cross declares Your astounding love. May our hearts and minds never stray from the foot of the cross, amen.

And you, being dead in your trespasses and the uncircumcision of your flesh, He has made alive together with Him, having forgiven you all trespasses, having wiped out the handwriting of requirements that was against us, which was contrary to us. And He has taken it out of the way, having nailed it to the cross.

Colossians 2:13–14

Beauty
AT THE
Foot of the Cross

Oh, where might the love of God be shown
In all its riches displayed,
Was there such a place in all the Earth
Divine love should be surveyed?
It was there on a hill outside the gate,
It was there, meant for all to see;
And love echoes 'cross the universe
From Jesus at Calvary.

IN THE EARLY 1900S, AN ASTRONOMER NAMED VESTO SLIPHER USED A telescope and a prism to observe the spectra of several bright galaxies, including the one pictured here: the magnificent Sombrero Galaxy (M104) in the constellation of Virgo. What he found were very recognizable line patterns—patterns reproducible in laboratories. These indicated the presence of specific atomic elements within the stars of the observed galaxies. The same signatures were also seen in light from the Sun. While the patterns themselves from these distant galaxies were identifiable, they were shifted toward the red side of their spectra compared with those from the laboratory or the Sun. At the time, it wasn't really understood that these galaxies *were* distant. Observations in the 1920s by Edwin Hubble showed that they were, and an important relationship was identified: the farther away a galaxy is, the more its light is "redshifted." This is now generally accepted as evidence that the universe is expanding. As the universe stretches, the wavelengths of light grow longer. Older, distant light is stretched the most, making it the reddest.

While the universe may be expanding, God is not. He has no spatial dimensions. He is both *transcendent*, meaning distinct from creation, and *omnipresent*, meaning everywhere present within it. He is as close to the distant galaxies as He is to our own neighborhoods, somehow separate from but present in His full Being in both. It is important to realize and appreciate that though fully present everywhere, He acts differently in different locations within space and time. We can understand this when we think of a verse like James 4:6: "Therefore it says, 'God opposes the proud, but gives grace to the humble.'" (ESV) He can be present to bless and oppose at the same time in different locations. All of this defies comprehension, but so does the expanding physical universe itself! The Lord stretched out the heavens. He is greater than all He has made, and He is present everywhere in His creation to rule and reign.

"Am I a God near at hand," says the LORD,
"And not a God afar off?
Can anyone hide himself in secret places,
So I shall not see him?" says the LORD;
"Do I not fill heaven and earth?" says the LORD.

Jeremiah 23:23–24

God is our refuge and strength,
A very present help in trouble.

Psalm 46:1

God's
Omnipresence

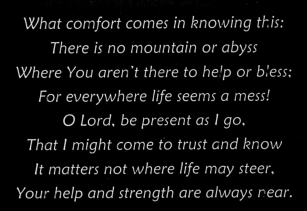

What comfort comes in knowing this:
There is no mountain or abyss
Where You aren't there to help or bless;
For everywhere life seems a mess!
O Lord, be present as I go,
That I might come to trust and know
It matters not where life may steer,
Your help and strength are always near.

GOD'S *Surprises*

Climb the rugged mountain;
Find a flower there.
Probe the deepest ocean;
See its creatures stare.
Magnify the atom;
Tell what parts there be.
Gaze ye into heaven;
God knows what you'll see!

Nature is full of unimaginable intricacies and surprises everywhere we look. Take any piece of God's creation—a leaf, a snowflake, a butterfly, even a single atom—and one could spend a lifetime studying the processes that shape and govern it. Who would have thought that immensely complex life could be found near scalding heat vents on the ocean floor, or high in the mountains where ice is as hard as a rock? Yet it's there and thriving—marvelously equipped by God to live in these desolate, harsh environments. So it shouldn't surprise us—yet it does nonetheless—to see such a strange and magnificently beautiful object as the Cat's Eye Nebula (NGC 6543) in our telescopes.

Located in the constellation Draco the Dragon, NGC 6543 is classified by astronomers as a *planetary nebula*. The term is historic rather than functional since these objects have nothing to do with planets. Using early, small telescopes, astronomers found their disclike shapes similar to that of the solar system planets—and hence the name was coined. Until very recently, planetary nebulae were thought to be relatively well-understood: shells of gas emitted from unstable stars. As repeated so often in the universe, however, reality is more exquisite and intricate than first thought. The complex dynamics of multiple, co-rotating, and outgassing stars with powerful radiation and sweeping magnetic fields are currently thought to be responsible for celestial masterpieces like the Cat's Eye.

While we should rightly praise God for His creativity seen so gloriously in nature, today's contemplation is a bit different. God would have you realize today that His creativity is not limited to the laws of physics or biology. If you have a problem, God has a solution—and probably not one you're expecting. Think of how He's remarkably provided for you in the past with people, places, and things at just the right time, in just the right way. Who among us would have picked a young shepherd, David, for a king? A path through the Red Sea to escape the Egyptians? A coin from a fish to pay the temple tax? A gruesome criminal's cross to redeem men? Yes, God has creative, marvelous plans to answer our every prayer. Lay your burdens at His feet, and watch what He does with them.

Behold, I am the Lord, the God of all flesh. Is there anything too hard for Me?

Jeremiah 32:27

Yes, and all who desire to live godly in Christ Jesus
will suffer persecution.

2 Timothy 3:12

LOCATED OFF THE TAIL OF THE BETTER-KNOWN CONSTELLATION LEO the Lion is the visually unremarkable constellation of Coma Berenices. If one is armed with a good-sized telescope, however, this area of the sky explodes with faint deep-sky treasures—mainly galaxies. One that's a favorite of amateur astronomers is the Black Eye Galaxy, M64. It appears like a real "shiner," with a dark dust band on one side silhouetted against a faint, glowing background. Remarkably, astronomers have discovered that the center part of the galaxy is rotating in the opposite direction of its outer dusty arms. This has led scientists to conclude that M64 was involved in an altercation with another smaller galaxy, which it now is in the process of absorbing.

As Christians, we're told plainly in Scripture that we'll suffer persecution for our faith. This will normally take the form of ridicule, slander, or shunning—but could possibly come in the form of verbal altercations, property damage, or physical harm. If we're to get a "black eye," however, let it be clearly for the cause of Christ—not our own sins of anger, contentiousness, pride, or revenge. Are you unfairly suffering right now at the hands of others? Much glory goes to God if you respond to this suffering righteously. Remember, vengeance belongs to God (Romans 12:19). Think, too, about the faithfulness of God over His creation, and follow the apostle Peter's admonition: "Let those who suffer according to the will of God commit their souls to Him in doing good, as to a faithful Creator" (1 Peter 4:19). And finally, remember the words of our Lord Jesus Himself and take courage: "Blessed are you when they revile and persecute you, and say all kinds of evil against you falsely for My sake. Rejoice and be exceedingly glad, for great is your reward in heaven, for so they persecuted the prophets who were before you" (Matthew 5:11–12).

But let none of you suffer as a murderer, a thief, an
evildoer, or as a busybody in other people's matters.
Yet if anyone suffers as a Christian, let him not be
ashamed, but let him glorify God in this matter.

1 Peter 4:15–16

THE
Way *to* Suffer

Lord, I'm suffering for You now;
Remember me as You allow
These circumstances in my life
Of unearned hurt, insult, and strife.

God, I need your Help today
And ask that for Your glory may
Respond in love to those who hate,
As Christ I seek to imitate.

The Last Day

Lesser sphere of darkest space,
Swing your mask across my face.
Note the startled humans glancing;
Fear they not the Day advancing?

"Immediately after the tribulation of those days the sun will be darkened, and the moon will not give its light; the stars will fall from heaven, and the powers of the heavens will be shaken. Then the sign of the Son of Man will appear in heaven, and then all the tribes of the earth will mourn, and they will see the Son of Man coming on the clouds of heaven with power and great glory."

Matthew 24:29–30

MARCH 7, 1970, 1:34 P.M., A STRANGE SENSATION FALLS OVER THE COUNTRYside. For three spectacular minutes, the midday Sun is eclipsed by the Moon and provides no more light than the full Moon itself at midnight.

The Moon's diameter is more than four hundred times smaller than the Sun's. That is roughly the same ratio as a soccer ball to a stadium. In God's providence, however, the much greater distance of the Sun makes it appear smaller so that the Moon's sphere perfectly fits like a mask over the Sun's face. This perfect match is very possibly unique among the solar system planets and their moons. Because of this amazing alignment, scientists have identified and studied the otherwise invisible outer atmosphere of the Sun called the *solar corona*. An understanding of this gaseous plasma may help in the prediction of climatic trends on Earth.

The temporary blocking of the Sun by the Moon during a total solar eclipse should not be cause for concern so much as for wonder. The book of Genesis makes clear, however, that God created the celestial lights for signs, not just for calendars. He used the starry skies to illustrate for Abraham how innumerable his descendants would be. The Bible also speaks plainly about a coming day of judgment by God, marked by signs in the heavens. To those who by faith are eagerly awaiting Him, this day will be one of unspeakable blessing. But to those who ignore or oppose Him, it is a day to be greatly feared.

Behold, the day of the LORD comes,
Cruel, with both wrath and fierce anger,
To lay the land desolate;
And He will destroy its sinners from it.
For the stars of heaven and their constellations
Will not give their light;
The sun will be darkened in its going forth,
And the moon will not cause its light to shine.

Isaiah 13:9–10

Now faith is the assurance of things hoped for, the
conviction of things not seen.

Hebrews 11:1 ESV

HAS SOMETHING BEAUTIFUL EVER LEFT YOU BREATHLESS? A glorious rainbow, a perfectly intricate snowflake, a colorful autumn forest, a mountaintop view on a clear day, the rising full Moon? Oh, how these scenes stick in our memories, making us hope to experience them again!

The Scriptures tell us that "hope deferred makes the heart sick, but a desire fulfilled is a tree of life" (Proverbs 13:12 ESV). Imagine what life will flood our souls when we gaze upon the Lord—our Blessed Hope—the source of all beauty. When we see His gracious countenance, cravings for any other created thing will disappear. Our deepest hope will be fulfilled. In that day, we will not need faith to convict our souls that He is true, for we will *see* Him. So it is that in heaven, faith and hope will pass away. But it's only there, in eternity, that we can experience the full measure of God's infinite love—timelessly ever new.

Praise You, Lord, for Your amazing love. Thank You for faith and hope that carry us through this life until we can see You and be with You in eternity. How we long for that day. "Maranatha," come, Lord Jesus!

For in this hope we were saved. Now hope that is seen is not hope. For who hopes for what he sees?

Romans 8:24 ESV

And now abide faith, hope, love, these three; but the greatest of these is love.

1 Corinthians 13:13

Barresi (INAF-IASF, Bologna, Italy), R. O'Connell (University of Virginia, Charlottesville), and the Wide Field Camera 3 Science Oversight Committee

WHERE *Beauty* GLEAMS WITH *Grace*

Where Beauty gleams with Grace
There is no further need for faith employed.
Fulfilled within that Face
The finest mortal hope is e'er enjoyed.
And love, desire of earthly hearts,
Has only there the means to be
The timeless giving birth
To all He covenants, eternally.

123

Alone
but Fruitful

Loneliness can take the joy of life away,
And forms a fertile soil for devils' lies to prey.
Look there, my soul, God's Word gives comfort to the one
Who joined with Christ, has timeless purpose just begun.

ON CLEAR AUTUMN NIGHTS IN THE NORTHERN HEMISPHERE, NEAR MID-night, a lone bright star can be seen skirting the horizon to the south. This is Fomalhaut, singularly bright in its whole quarter of the sky. It is in the faint constellation of Piscis Austrinus, the Southern Fish. *Fomalhaut* is Arabic, meaning "mouth of the whale," and it is a very old name. This constellation was one of forty-eight listed by Ptolemy in the second century—a list compiled from even more ancient records. Fomalhaut is only twenty-five light-years distant; hence, it is relatively close to our solar system. It is about twice as large and massive as the Sun. Though seemingly isolated, it is believed by some to be part of a group of sixteen stars called the Castor Moving Group, an association of stars traveling together in the same direction across the sky.

Fomalhaut has a prominent place in modern astronomy as well as ancient lore. The first planet outside our solar system ever to be directly imaged and confirmed was discovered on the inner edge of a very large dusty ring around the star. From the effect of its gravity on the ring, scientists believe the planet is no larger than three times the size of Jupiter. Though it is a billion times fainter than its star, it daily reflects a bit of Fomalhaut's bright light to us.

Are you ever lonely? Do you feel out of place, ineffective, unnoticed, or unproductive? The Lord wants to encourage you today. He does not like His people to be isolated. He has others nearby who share your values and interests; ask Him to make them known. Though you feel like a lone star, know that God in His providence and kindness is working His purposes in and through you. He has redeemed you with the blood of His own Son and placed His Spirit within you. The light of Christ that emanates from you now will unquestionably affect others for good, even if you don't see evidence of it right away. Hold fast to your faith; in Christ, your life has eternal purpose—and you are never alone.

Do not let the son of the foreigner
Who has joined himself to the LORD
Speak, saying,
"The LORD has utterly separated me from His people". . . .
Even to them I will give in My house
And within My walls a place and a name
Better than that of sons and daughters;
I will give them an everlasting name
That shall not be cut off.

Isaiah 56:3, 5

THY Kingdom Come

What matter is so strange as this,
At once both near, yet far away?
I think upon His kingdom come,
And watch intently for the Day.

"The time is fulfilled, and the kingdom of God
is at hand. Repent, and believe in the gospel."

Mark 1:15

ONE OF THE BRIGHTEST COMETS TO APPEAR IN THE LAST HALF OF THE twentieth century, Comet Hyakutake was seen by city dwellers as a diffuse, hazy blob in the springtime sky of 1996. But for those living in more rural areas, this celestial spectacle will not be soon forgotten. Visually equal in size to the Big Dipper, Hyakutake's long single tail swept straight back from its head, or *coma*, which itself appeared as large as the full Moon. The comet's remarkable appearance was due to its "close" passage to Earth rather than its actual size, which was quite small. Passing only 9 million miles away, this encounter was at only one-tenth of the distance between Earth and the Sun. Had Comet Hale-Bopp—an intrinsically much larger comet—passed this close, it would have easily been seen in broad daylight.

Many theologians today describe the kingdom of God as the "already, but not yet." This paradoxically describes the fact that with the beginning of Christ's church, certain aspects of His ultimate kingdom—such as joy, peace, fellowship, and righteous living—have already begun. The true fulfillment of the kingdom, however, won't occur until the King Himself—the Lord Jesus Christ—returns. Comet Hyakutake passed "close" to Earth, when in reality it was still millions of miles away. Likewise, God's kingdom is "at hand," just as Christ taught, yet still some distance away.

O Lord, may Your kingdom come—and come completely. Even a tiny glimpse of it makes us long for more. Come with the clouds so that every eye may see You. How we eagerly wait for and desire to hasten the day of Your return (2 Peter 3:12).

For our citizenship is in heaven,
from which we also eagerly wait for
the Savior, the Lord Jesus Christ.

Philippians 3:20

Have you ever stumbled in the dark? Perhaps you've tripped coming into the house when the front light is off or fallen over a slipper when the bedroom is black. Tripping and slipping are seldom pleasurable and can cause significant hurt! Our contemplation today is taken from Isaiah 26: "The path of the righteous is level" (v. 7). God's promise to us is that by following Him, our feet will miss many of the problems in life that trip others up. Dishonesty, unfaithfulness, unchecked bitterness . . . these all lead to broken, painful relationships that make life hard. But these actions should not characterize the life of God's redeemed. That is not to say that everything in our lives will go smoothly. On the contrary, we can predict that it won't. God sends trials into our lives to reveal to us the genuineness of our faith; to show us again His power and purpose to deliver us; to collect praise on the day Christ returns—both from believers and unbelievers (1 Peter 1:7).

"In the path of your judgments, O Lord, we wait for you" (Isaiah 26:8). Waiting honors God. We wait *in* His paths, not *off* them. We yearn for Him "in the night" (v. 9). While *night* implies spiritual and emotional darkness, perhaps Isaiah simply means it literally. Maybe tonight—as we've long promised ourselves—we will actually go for a walk beneath the stars and spend time with the Lord. In that hour, we can contemplate His amazing universe and think again on His power and promises. Perhaps tonight we will even hear His voice, for His Word says: "When I thought, 'My foot slips,' your steadfast love, O Lord, held me up. When the cares of my heart are many, your consolations cheer my soul" (Psalm 94:18–19 esv).

Thank You, Lord, for Your faithfulness and promises. Thank You for leading me on a level path. I know You will bring back the light of day though all right now is dark. You are my hope; I trust You, amen.

The path of the righteous is level;
you make level the way of the righteous.
In the path of your judgments,
O Lord, we wait for you;
your name and remembrance
are the desire of our soul.
My soul yearns for you in the night;
my spirit within me earnestly seeks you.

Isaiah 26:7 esv

Yearning for God in the Night

It's night, O Lord, and You I seek;
No other god will do.
'Tis You who formed the stars I see;
Your help I now pursue.
Lord, may I hear that gracious voice
In love You guarantee;
But meanwhile I will walk secure,
For You have ransomed me.

Fighting WITH THE *Unseen*

One world is immaterial,
One such, that human eye can see.
Indeed the more ethereal
Directs the latter's destiny.

> But Paul, greatly annoyed, turned and
> said to the spirit, "I command you in
> the name of Jesus Christ to come out of
> her." And he came out that very hour.

Acts 16:18

NASA, ESA, J. Clarke (Boston University), and Z. Levay (STScI)

Resist the devil and he will flee from you.

James 4:7

THIS GLORIOUS IMAGE OF THE PLANET SATURN WAS TAKEN BY NASA's Hubble Space Telescope. The telescope's camera used a detector that allows it to "see" not only visible light wavelengths, but also any ultraviolet light coming from the planet. Use of this detector revealed the otherwise invisible ring of light (similar to Earth's auroras) pictured here around Saturn's southern pole. We can't see ultraviolet light with our unaided eyes, so what color is it? Image processing experts rendered it blue, thereby communicating visually that it is on the blue end of the electromagnetic spectrum, opposite from red. In fact, there are many forms of light beyond detection with our eyes, which are just as "real" as the light we see. Those with wavelengths shorter than violet can hurt us, such as ultraviolet light, X-rays, and gamma rays.

God's universe contains many spiritual beings and forces at work that we don't see—some are good and others can hurt us. But just as the Lord uses the atmosphere and magnetic field of the Earth to protect us from harmful radiation, so He also uses His Name and Word to protect us from unseen evil forces. Knowing the Scriptures well protects our minds and hearts from the devil's lies. Even Jesus quoted Scripture to resist the devil, since the Word of God is "the sword of the Spirit" (Ephesians 6:17). Likewise, we possess authority in the name of Jesus to resist and put to flight the spiritual powers that oppose us.

If your mind is unusually full of temptations, or your work for the Lord is strangely frustrated or jeopardized, engage the unseen forces around you with the weapons God has provided. Someone's eternal destiny may be at stake. "For the weapons of our warfare are not carnal but mighty in God for pulling down strongholds, casting down arguments and every high thing that exalts itself against the knowledge of God, bringing every thought into captivity to the obedience of Christ" (2 Corinthians 10:4–5).

Then Jesus said to him, "Be gone, Satan! For it is written, 'You shall worship the Lord your God and him only shall you serve.'"

Matthew 4:10 ESV

It's futile to try to comprehend the power of God. Scripture tells us that His power is without measure. In Job 26, we are called to consider how He created the universe from nothing; how He controls the powers of sea, sky, and nature; and how the pillars of heaven itself tremble with His mere voice. All of this is summarized in verse 14 as "the mere edges of His ways."

Looking to the heavens, we sense His power in objects like the particle beam of Galaxy M87, pictured here, which is accelerating electrons and other sub-atomic particles trillions upon trillions of miles across space at speeds approaching that of light. The colossal jet is thought to be powered by a black hole at the center of M87 that has more than 2 billion times the mass of the Sun. Astronomers believe that such massive black holes exist at the cores of most galaxies, each spinning hundreds of billions of stars in orbit around them in their immense, unyielding gravitational clutches. Regarding the immeasurable heavens, Psalm 33:9 reminds us that the Lord created them with a word: "For He spoke, and it was done; He commanded, and it stood fast."

O Lord, we kneel in weakness and awe before You. How infinite You are in strength, wisdom, and majesty! Let our souls remember Your greatness as we live out our days. Thank You for Your unspeakably grand creation and for Your even more glorious redemption. You are great and greatly to be praised!

And I heard, as it were, the voice of a great multitude, as the sound of many waters and as the sound of mighty thunderings, saying, "Alleluia! For the Lord God Omnipotent reigns!"

Revelation 19:6

He stretches out the north over empty space;
He hangs the earth on nothing.
He binds up the water in His thick clouds,
Yet the clouds are not broken under it.
He covers the face of His throne,
And spreads His cloud over it.
He drew a circular horizon on the face of the waters,
At the boundary of light and darkness.
The pillars of heaven tremble,
And are astonished at His rebuke.
He stirs up the sea with His power,
And by His understanding He breaks up the storm.
By His Spirit He adorned the heavens;
His hand pierced the fleeing serpent.
Indeed these are the mere edges of His ways,
And how small a whisper we hear of Him!
But the thunder of His power who can understand?

Job 26:7–14

GOD
Omnipotent

What power can human feebleness e'en entertain?
That we should think to comprehend the strength of God
Makes credible the hope of any lowly ant
To trek its way across the stacked assembly of
The planet's books, and thereby realize their sense.
O Lord, such foolish pretense we will not embrace,
But rather with our faces bowed in worship here
Give praise to God omnipotent,
The One whom angels fear.

Let the sea roar, and all its fullness,
The world and those who dwell in it;
Let the rivers clap their hands;
Let the hills be joyful together before the Lord,
For He is coming to judge the earth.
With righteousness He shall judge the world,
And the peoples with equity.

Psalm 98:7–9

***

Our Earth circles the Sun in very nearly the same geometric plane as the Sun's equator. But we're not rotating "straight up" in this plane, like a well-spinning toy top on the floor. Instead, our poles are tipped over 23.5 degrees. Thus, in the summer months, we're tipped toward the Sun and our days are longer than our nights. Likewise, in the winter months, we're tipped away from the Sun and nights are longer. The midpoints—when the lengths of day and night are equal—are called the *equinoxes*. There is one in spring and one in autumn. In Roman times, the Sun passed through the stars we now call the constellation of Libra during the autumnal equinox. Hence the Romans viewed this constellation as two scales measuring equality—though there's no evident star pattern that would cause you to visualize this. It was later considered the "Scales of Justice" held by Julius Caesar or, alternatively, by Virgo—the Roman goddess of justice. Interestingly, the constellation also represented scales to the ancient Babylonians. It was held sacred in their myth of the Sun god Shamash, the patron of truth and justice. Libra is the only constellation in which the Sun and planets appear that is not associated with a living thing (like an animal, human, or mythological beast).

Psalm 97:2 tells us that righteousness and justice are the foundation of God's throne. These are two important and unchanging attributes of God. Justice will indeed come from the heavens—from the very throne of heaven. It will be meted out by the Lord on the "great and dreadful" Day of Judgment (Malachi 4:5). The judgments of God revealed on that day will be so astounding that even nature itself will rejoice at them (Psalm 98:7–8).

Do you love justice? Do you treat others equally? Do you live with an awareness that the great Day is coming and that you will be judged for how your life is spent? Take these various thoughts to heart today, and ask the God of Justice—the *Elohay Mishpat*—to help you love what He loves and hate what He hates.

Justice

For those who place their faith in Christ,
One scale we should not fear:
His righteousness weighed 'gainst our sins
Will tip the balance clear.
Yet Jesus taught that we will see
Rewards for what we do.
Let us delight in justice, then,
And righteousness pursue.

Christ,
Our Bridegroom

What picture this, that testifies in time
Of things so grand, sheer time cannot contain,
And manifests a unity sublime
Mere mortal consummations fail attain?
These earthly vows reflect the Mind of Love,
Which set eternity to be their end—
Depicting here the joyful world above,
Where faithfulness on flesh will ne'er depend.
A picture true, yet muted tint of truth,
The order of Earth's partners rightly made,
No better than the faded print of youth
To represent maturity conveyed.

This picture His, its virtues fully shown,
When Christ Himself shall marry those His own.

*Let us be glad and rejoice and give Him glory, for the marriage of
the Lamb has come, and His wife has made herself ready.*

Revelation 19:7

THERE'S A BEAUTIFUL CELESTIAL RING IN THE SKY THAT CAN REMIND US OF
our glorious future as members of the church, the bride of Christ. It's
M57, the Ring Nebula, one of many objects called planetary nebulae due
to their disclike shapes. Such nebulae are actually glowing gases emitted
and radiated by their central stars. The physics involved are very complex.
The varying characteristics of the central star, or stars, such as mass, temperature, and spin, result in many varieties of these nebulae.

More amazing than any celestial object, however, is the celestial marriage feast God is planning for Christ and His church. The apostle Paul
tells us in Ephesians 5 that earthly marriage is really a picture—albeit par-
tial—of that glorious and mysterious heavenly relationship that will be
ours in Christ. Are you sad because you are currently unmarried? Take
heart; you are deeply beloved of God. Even the Lord Jesus remained single
here—but your marriage date in heaven is already set (along with His) as
surely as the Word of God itself is true. How wonderfully rich it is that
John the Baptist used the illustration of the Bridegroom to describe Christ
(John 3:29). Even richer is the fact that Christ used the same metaphor in
describing Himself (Mark 2:19–20). Finally, contemplate the indescribable promise made by God to us, His redeemed people: "And as the
bridegroom rejoices over the bride, so shall your God rejoice over you"
(Isaiah 62:5).

*For no one ever hated his own flesh, but nourishes and
cherishes it, just as the Lord does the church. For we are
members of His body, of His flesh and of His bones.
"For this reason a man shall leave his father and
mother and be joined to his wife, and the two shall
become one flesh." This is a great mystery, but I speak
concerning Christ and the church.*

Ephesians 5:29–32

The Great Red Spot on Jupiter is an immense, swirling high pressure storm, located twenty-two degrees south of Jupiter's equator. It is somewhat akin to a hurricane on Earth but with much higher wind speeds. Earth's typhoons and hurricanes generally have sustained winds under 150 miles per hour. The very highest on record were 190. The Great Red Spot's winds are around 265 miles per hour—twice that of a strong Category 3 Atlantic hurricane. The Spot is also unimaginably large, large enough to swallow three whole Earths! Because of its immense size, it takes a full six Earth days to complete one rotation. Most remarkably though, it was reportedly seen first in the seventeenth century, making it at least three hundred years old—and possibly much older.

Do you know what it's like to be caught in the vortex of anger? Like Jupiter's dense atmosphere, in those moments our minds are clouded and spin ferociously with high-velocity defensive arguments. Perhaps we've been wrongly criticized, producing within us an intense desire to set the record straight or point out the many deficiencies of those who criticized us. Thoughts and counter thoughts can rage in our souls for days and, if not tended to, can lead to bitterness that can last for years—maybe even for a lifetime. The gospel can break this cycle and bring peace. It reminds us that in the flesh we are actually worse than anyone's most accurate criticism. Our sins required the very blood of Christ to wash them away. Scripture tells us that we were spiritually dead and enemies of God before His grace took hold in our lives.

If you are tempted to anger, slow down. Remind yourself that God opposes the proud but gives grace to the humble, and remember your dire state without His grace. Then choose to deal with others as He has dealt with you. Christ calmed the storm on the sea of Galilee with these words: "Peace, be still!" (Mark 4:39). Embrace God's Word from Psalm 46:10, even though the sea is raging and your mountains are trembling: "Be still, and know that I am God." He can and will help you; He wants to. For His glory, sow peace, and you will reap peace.

Therefore be imitators of God, as beloved children. And walk in love, as Christ loved us and gave himself up for us.

Ephesians 5:1–2 ESV

Finally, brothers, rejoice. Aim for restoration, comfort one another, agree with one another, live in peace; and the God of love and peace will be with you.

2 Corinthians 13:11 ESV

Anger swirls in ways that won't abate;
Lengthy are the years it blusters like a storm.
Better then to keep the temper straight,
Humbly letting gospel truth your course inform.

ANGER

Tʜᴇʀᴇ's ᴀ ᴘᴀɪʀ ᴏꜰ ꜰᴀɪɴᴛ, ɢʜᴏsᴛʟʏ ɴᴇʙᴜʟᴀᴇ ɪɴ ᴛʜᴇ sᴜᴍᴍᴇʀ sᴋʏ ᴛʜᴀᴛ ᴀʀᴇ favorite viewing targets for amateur astronomers. Collectively known as the Veil Nebula, they are located in the constellation of Cygnus the Swan—popularly called the Northern Cross. Sensitive wide-field photos reveal that the two segments are part of the same system that forms—along with other smaller pieces—a vast celestial ring. The nebula is the remains of a star that exploded thousands of years ago, ripping itself to shreds and shooting material outward in every direction. The image here shows one segment.

As believers, we're reminded of another veil torn in two: the great veil of the Jewish temple, separating the Holy Place from the Most Holy Place. It was miraculously torn from top to bottom at the death of Christ, signifying that now we—through the righteousness and sacrifice of Christ—have access to the very seat of holiness: God Himself. In chapter after chapter, the author of Hebrews details for us how the Old Testament sacrificial system, with its high priests and slaughtered animals, has its ultimate fulfillment in Jesus, who is both the eternal High Priest and the spotless sacrificial Lamb. This is explained in great detail so that we might have hope.

Are you in a situation that appears hopeless? Think again of God's meticulously planned work of salvation. Think how faithful He was in keeping His promise of a Savior and how He has orchestrated every aspect of His loving plan to save us. The same faithful God has a plan at work for your life as well. Trust Him to bring it to pass, for "If God is for us, who can be against us? He who did not spare His own Son, but delivered Him up for us all, how shall He not with Him also freely give us all things?" (Romans 8:31–32).

Therefore, brethren, having boldness to enter the Holiest by the blood of Jesus, by a new and living way which He consecrated for us, through the veil, that is, His flesh, and having a High Priest over the house of God, let us draw near with a true heart in full assurance of faith, having our hearts sprinkled from an evil conscience and our bodies washed with pure water. Let us hold fast the confession of our hope without wavering, for He who promised is faithful.

Hebrews 10:19–23

Michael W. Carer, M.D.

The Veil

His body torn—just as He said—
And raised to life up from the dead;
When pressed so hard I cannot cope,
Faithful Jesus gives me hope.

He Who Places Faith in *Jesus*

He who places faith in Jesus
Gains a hope that cannot fail.
Weak and brokenhearted souls will
Through God's faithfulness prevail.
Rise up to embrace His promise;
He works only what is right.
Joy returns unto the righteous;
Into darkness, He brings light.

Faithful love He keeps forever;
Mercies new appear each day.
By His Spirit, through His people,
Grace will carry griefs away.
Lift your heart to study Jesus;
He has walked this way before.
Painful loss came to the Savior,
Yet He trusted God the more.

We, the sheep, have Him as Shepherd!
He will guide us day and night.
Worry lurks at ev'ry turn but
Perfect Love dismisses fright.
Place His loving yoke upon you;
Know His presence at your side.
He will help you through the trouble;
Ev'ry step, Himself provide.

Then Jesus spoke to them again, saying,
"I am the light of the world. He who
follows Me shall not walk in darkness,
but have the light of life."

John 8:12

Have you recently suffered a significant loss? Perhaps a loved one is no longer nearby, or some unforeseen event has caused such pain or grief that you're truly brokenhearted. If so, in God's providence, today's contemplation is especially for you. Today, hear this undeniable truth: God brings light into darkness. It belongs to God to do this. He did it on the very first day; His starry heavens make glorious the pitch black of outer space. And He will most assuredly shine His light into your soul once again.

Jesus is our brother in affliction. As Isaiah 53:4 says, "Surely He has borne our griefs and carried our sorrows." He understands firsthand your heartache, and it is He who will never leave nor forsake you. Though you are weak, He is both strong and faithful, and His love cannot fail. Yoke your heart to Him—His oxlike strength will pull you through this sad and painful time, step by step. Look there—even now His light begins to shine.

Do not rejoice over me, my enemy;
When I fall, I will arise;
When I sit in darkness,
The Lord will be a light to me.

Micah 7:8

Unto the upright there
arises light in the darkness.

Psalm 112:4

IN GENESIS 1:14, WE READ THAT THE LORD CREATED THE SUN, MOON, AND stars not only to provide light upon Earth, but that they could be used for "signs and seasons, and for days and years." If you pause to think about it, our twenty-four-hour day, 365-day year, and four seasons are all anchored in how the Earth interacts with the Sun. In Europe and America, even the seven days of the week are named after the seven brightest moving objects in the sky. But what about *signs*? What does this mean? We can discern at least three categories of *signs*: celestial signposts for the seasons, ways for God to illustrate something, and predictive indicators.

In the first category, rural peoples who are accustomed to looking at the stars can tell when the next season is approaching even if temperatures haven't changed. Seeing the bright star Capella, for example, signals that the winter season is just around the corner. In the second category, the Lord uses the stars in His Word to illustrate His power, the height of His love, and the faithfulness of His promises. He promised Abraham, for instance, that his descendents would be as numerous as the stars in the sky.

In the third category, the Lord uses the heavens to provide signs of His coming. The star of Bethlehem is an example, as well as the Moon turning to blood (red) in Acts 2:20. This, of course, happens naturally during a lunar eclipse, when the Moon passes into Earth's shadow and is only illuminated by the red wavelengths that are bent onto its face after passing through the Earth's atmosphere. The apostle Peter, quoting the prophet Joel, witnessed to those at Pentecost about Christ by referring to the sign of the blood Moon. Astronomers can verify that on April 3, AD 33, the rising Moon over Jerusalem was in eclipse. This is one of two possible dates during the reign of Pontius Pilate in Jerusalem when the Passover fell on Friday, the preparation day for the Sabbath. This important detail regarding the timing of Jesus' death as recorded in the New Testament gives witness to the truth of God's Word. That is, there is good evidence that the Moon rose red over Jerusalem on Good Friday.

Lord, how we marvel at Your wisdom, understanding, and might. We praise You for the accuracy and help of Your amazing Word, amen.

The sun shall be turned into darkness,
And the moon into blood,
Before the coming of the great and awesome day of the LORD.
And it shall come to pass
That whoever calls on the name of the LORD
Shall be saved.

Acts 2:20–21

Signs

Lord, how Your greatness fills my heart
To tell of all that You impart
In truth and how this is conferred
To those who linger in Your Word.
Because of You, we apprehend
Reality and comprehend
That starry signs You give to men
Can help them to be born again.

FAINT, CLEAR,
& *Beautiful*

Kevin Hartnett

See our Lord, His image plainly shown;
On every page, rich symbols brought to view,
Sweet pictures of the gospel there made known,
The whispers of His love, ours to review.

HAVE YOU EVER NOTICED A FAINT GLOW COMING FROM THE "DARK" SIDE OF the Moon? Since direct sunlight can't illuminate this part of its sphere, it ought to be jet-black. So what's going on here? Where's this light coming from? The answer is curious and fun to know: this faint glow is sunlight that's first been reflected from Earth. It's called Earthshine; it is light from the Sun that's been reflected from the cloud tops of Earth to the Moon, where it has bounced back to Earth for us to view. The brightness of this glow depends on how much cloud cover there is here on Earth.

Astronomers have recently taken a new interest in this phenomenon. Since it's essentially a reflection of Earth's light, Earthshine provides scientists a way to "see" Earth from the vantage point of space. This is helpful because, by examining the spectrum of this light, astronomers have a means of knowing what a life-bearing planet "looks like" spectroscopically. If a similar spectroscopic signature should ever be seen from another planet, it would obviously generate a lot of interest!

As we read through the Old Testament, a faint, clear, and beautiful image of our Savior appears where we might not have expected it. Perhaps it's simply because we've not been trained to look for it there, but it brings glory to God as we realize the many ways that the Old Testament points to Christ. We think of the bronze serpent lifted up on a pole for healing amid the Israelite camp (Numbers 21:9); the Passover lamb, whose blood caused the Angel of Death to pass over a believer's house (Exodus 12); the ram, caught by its head in thorns, provided by God as a substitute for the sacrificial offering of Isaac (Genesis 22); the male lamb without blemish used as a sin offering (Leviticus 1); the kinsman-redeemer of the book of Ruth (Ruth 4); the rock from which sprang life-giving water (Exodus 17); the One whose hands and feet were pierced (Psalm 22); the arm of the Lord (Isaiah 53); and the list goes on and on.

Lord, please open our eyes to see our precious Lord Jesus in the pages of the Old Testament. How we thrill at each new glimpse of Your timeless, redeeming love. And how we delight to see His faint, clear, and beautiful image there, amen.

And beginning at Moses and all the Prophets, He expounded to them in all the Scriptures the things concerning Himself.

Luke 24:27

God, Our Help

When my problems seem beyond repair,
Stubborn troubles all that I can see,
Jesus gives great cause for hopeful prayer:
He who made the heavens cares for me.

KING DAVID PENNED THIS STATEMENT OF TRUST IN PSALM 121:1–2: "I will lift up my eyes to the hills—from whence comes my help? My help comes from the LORD, who made heaven and earth." Perhaps today you just need help. Circumstances have conspired to strain your relationships, beat you down, and remove what little joy you had. Maybe it's the pain in your body, stress over the children, or dwindling finances. It's hard to concentrate, as everything looks horribly black, with little hope of change. If this is the case, take your lead from David. He certainly knew troubles—in his family, in his army, and in his kingdom. What gave David hope was that the God who made the heavens and the Earth was also his refuge and strength.

Think again of the heavens: immense, dazzling stars; colossal galaxies; powerful supernovae. These all exist at His pleasure. He spoke them into existence and will extinguish them just as easily. He is almighty. He brings light into darkness and makes springs of water flow in the desert (Psalm 107:35). There is nothing too difficult for Him.

Troubles take many forms, and God works divine purposes through them that we don't always immediately understand. But He couldn't be our Deliverer unless there were things to deliver us from, and He receives great glory when we trust Him in the face of difficulties. The book of Job reveals clearly that this is so. Honor Him by trusting in His love today. He is the Good Shepherd. He knows how to help and protect His sheep. He knows how to help and protect *you*.

I would have despaired unless
I had believed that I would
see the goodness of the LORD
in the land of the living.

Psalm 27:13 NASB

Acknowledgment: D. Goulermis (Max-Planck Institute for Astronomy, Heidelberg)

AMONG THE CATEGORIES OF ASTRONOMICAL OBJECTS IS A GROUP CALLED *brown dwarfs*. These are bodies more massive than planets, but not massive enough to produce the heat necessary to ignite the process of nuclear fusion that causes stars to shine. They are basically failed stars. Planets are generally cool objects. For smaller, rocky ones like Earth, their heat comes mainly from the stars they orbit. Larger, gaseous ones like Jupiter emit some internal heat of their own—generated from the slow contraction of their material—but they are still relatively cool. Stars, of course, are remarkably hot. The interior temperature of the Sun is around 27 million degrees Fahrenheit! But brown dwarfs are in between. They're not really normal planets but not normal stars either. In fact, they are hard to observe and classify because they are small, shine only faintly, and have characteristics that make them difficult to distinguish from small stars.

All this brings to mind God's stern but loving warning to the church of the Laodiceans. God wants us individually and as churches to be clearly distinguishable as Christians. If your love for God is only lukewarm and your fulfillment is in earthly things rather than in Him, examine the genuineness of your faith. God stands at the door of your heart knocking. What you consider life-giving is a facade. Look at those around you who are truly content, and see that they are fulfilled because their lives have been dramatically changed by the gospel of Jesus.

Do you know what the gospel is? If not, today the Lord is calling to you. Ask Him to show you why it's phenomenally good news that Christ died. Read the Bible, and ask others who have done so to tell you what they've learned.

If you're lukewarm toward the Lord
While others seem so hot,
Ask the Holy Spirit why
They are, but you are not.
It may be you've never learned
Why Christ came forth to die.
The "greatest story ever told"
Should make your love leap high.

Lukewarm

"And to the angel of the church of the Laodiceans write, 'These things says the Amen, the Faithful and True Witness, the Beginning of the creation of God: "I know your works, that you are neither cold nor hot. I could wish you were cold or hot. So then, because you are lukewarm, and neither cold nor hot, I will vomit you out of My mouth. Because you say, 'I am rich, have become wealthy, and have need of nothing'—and do not know that you are wretched, miserable, poor, blind, and naked—I counsel you to buy from Me gold refined in the fire, that you may be rich; and white garments, that you may be clothed, that the shame of your nakedness may not be revealed; and anoint your eyes with eye salve, that you may see. As many as I love, I rebuke and chasten. Therefore be zealous and repent. Behold, I stand at the door and knock. If anyone hears My voice and opens the door, I will come in to him and dine with him, and he with Me. To him who overcomes I will grant to sit with Me on My throne, as I also overcame and sat down with My Father on His throne. "He who has an ear, let him hear what the Spirit says to the churches."'"

Revelation 3:14–22

REDEMPTION FROM SLAVERY, ADOPTION INTO A FAMILY, MARRIAGE—WHAT WONDER-fully rich, yet gloriously true metaphors the Lord uses to describe His amazing love for us. Today—yes even today—amidst all your hurt, hardship, and fatigue, think on these truths. They will revive your soul to the point of overflowing praise.

Were we not all slaves—sold into the bondage of selfish living, not thinking about God or serving Him, but making a daily mess of our relationships, our bodies, and our futures? Yet the Lord Jesus intervened. He found us standing chained, ill-clothed, weak, and helpless upon the devil's awful bidding block, and He bought us back. He rescued us from hell itself, purchasing us with the great price of His own blood—not because we were inherently worth the price, but because it was the only price that could free us.

And once bought, we've been brought into His home, treated like the returning Prodigal Son, made heirs of eternal life and every spiritual blessing in the heavenly places in Christ. We can address God now as Abba, Father, ever-approachable, ever-loving, ever-knowing, ever-powerful.

And if all this were not enough, He now covenants with us as a Groom does with His beloved bride, to love her and cherish her as long as He lives. He plans a marriage feast. The angels are celebrating even now. There's laughter coming, fulfillment, and tremendous eternal joy.

Now these things may all seem so amazing that they're hard to believe. But why? Why shouldn't God's love be amazing beyond belief, just as He Himself is beyond measure and estimation in every way? His love is not like ours, just as we creatures—though made in His image—are really not much like the great Creator at all. Our love is fickle and laced with selfishness. His isn't. He is incapable of sin or faithlessness. His love is all that love can ever be, for He is Love.

So it's not surprising that He uses the height of the heavens to illustrate His love. Trillions upon trillions upon trillions of miles high—so great is His love toward those who fear Him. And as cosmic as it is in measure, it is even more so in scope. God Himself, bound within His own righteousness to uphold Justice by judging sin, found a way to free us from our rightful punishment. Love Himself became incarnate and hung in our place on the cross. God's sacrificial provision of Christ satisfied His own demand to uphold righteousness. Mercy triumphed over judgment. Praise the Lord!

For as high as the heavens are above the earth, so great is his steadfast love toward those who fear him.

Psalm 103:11 ESV

For God so loved the world that He gave His only begotten Son, that whoever believes in Him should not perish but have everlasting life.

John 3:16

Love

Love, the soul's true satisfaction,
Love much higher than the skies;
Love came at the call of Justice;
Love was cruelly crucified.

CHRIST, the Center

Do you know the order of the planets?
Can you tell the clockwork in their circling?
Neither has man fully seen creation
Centered on the glory of the Son.

*He is the image of the invisible God, the firstborn over
all creation. For by Him all things were created that are
in heaven and that are on earth, visible and invisible,
whether thrones or dominions or principalities or
powers. All things were created through Him and for
Him. And He is before all things, and in Him all
things consist. And He is the head of the body, the
church, who is the beginning, the firstborn from the
dead, that in all things He may have the preeminence.*

Colossians 1:15–18

THIS AMAZING IMAGE OF JUPITER AND ITS MOON IO WAS TAKEN BY
NASA's *Cassini* spacecraft as it passed by the giant planet in
January 2001 on its way to Saturn. Io is one of the four large Galilean
moons of Jupiter, so named because they were discovered by Galileo
in the early seventeenth century using the newly invented technol-
ogy of his day—the telescope! Galileo's discovery convincingly
demonstrated that Earth was not the center of every astronomical
body's sphere of motion. This was an important argument in per-
suading the scientific authorities of his day to accept that the Sun,
not Earth, was the center of the solar system. While this seems elementary to us today, this was not man's understanding for most of
recorded history. From their perspective, the planets seemed to zig-
zag across the night sky from month to month. Astronomers now
know that the Sun is indeed the center of the solar system and that
all the planets, including Earth, move in great elliptically shaped
orbits around it.

The Scriptures make it clear that all things in heaven and on Earth
are to be summed up in God's glorious Son, the Lord Jesus Christ.
History is moving unalterably toward this culmination. One day, we
will see much more clearly how God's desire to glorify His Son drives
all of created history. He will be exalted above every name that is
named. He will banish Satan and his legions to the lake of fire, and
He will take His church—purchased with His own blood—as His
bride. Does this perspective guide your thinking and living? Is Christ
the center of your life?

THE ENGLISH WORD *ASTRONOMY* IS DERIVED FROM TWO GREEK WORDS: *astro* meaning "star" and *nomos* meaning "law" or "arrangement." Astronomy, then, is literally the study of the laws that govern the order and arrangement of the stars. There are many of these laws, from simple ones like "stars rise in the east and set in the west," to more complex ones like "the brightness of a star is inversely proportional to its distance squared." What they all have in common is that they are based on the fundamental laws of physics that govern the material universe. We expect that the planets will stay in their obits because they must inevitably obey the laws of gravity, conservation of energy, angular momentum, and the like. Humans, on the other hand, can choose whether or not they obey certain physical laws. Willfully violating the laws of physics, however, results in sure consequences—here on Earth, it can mean broken bones or hospital visits!

God's Word is full of spiritual laws that are just as true and reliable as the physical ones. Think of them all: "The fear of the LORD is the beginning of wisdom" (Psalm 111:10); "Give, and it will be given to you" (Luke 6:38); "He who walks with wise men will become wise" (Proverbs 13:20); and "Whatever a man sows, that he will also reap" (Galatians 6:7). Think of all the principles Jesus taught in Matthew 5 at the Sermon on the Mount: "Blessed are the poor in spirit, for theirs is the kingdom of heaven . . . Blessed are the meek . . . Blessed are the peacemakers." We see that the spiritual laws of the kingdom are often contrary to the wisdom of this world: "Love your enemies . . . and pray for those who spitefully use you and persecute you" (Matthew 5:44); "Whoever exalts himself will be humbled, and he who humbles himself will be exalted" (23:12); and "Better is a dinner of herbs where love is, than a fatted calf with hatred" (Proverbs 15:17). In our flesh, we may not be inclined to follow these spiritual laws naturally—but if we do, we will surely see them deliver what they promise. May God give us wisdom today to see, appreciate, and obey the spiritual laws that He's ordained in His universe. May we also, out of love for Him, study His Word to better learn the principles that please Him and magnify His name.

"But he who is greatest among you shall be your servant.
And whoever exalts himself will be humbled, and he who
humbles himself will be exalted."

Matthew 23:11–12

PHYSICAL
AND
SPIRITUAL LAWS

Laws that govern stars, you see,
Teachers call astronomy;
Finding truth for living brings
Also rules for heavenly things.

No Hiding

Lord, You know my good and bad;
Every thought, Your "eyes" can "see,"
Let my worship make You glad, as
Nothing e'er is hid from Thee.

As these two adjacent images from the Hubble Space Telescope beautifully illustrate, observing the heavens in various wavelengths of light can reveal remarkably different things. This is because electromagnetic radiation (that is, "light" across the full range of the spectrum including X-ray, ultraviolet, infrared, and radio waves) interacts with the physical size and atomic composition of the objects that it strikes. If you've ever lost reception on an AM radio station driving under a bridge, but not an FM one, you've experienced this principle. The lower frequency, longer wavelength AM signal gets reflected by the overpass, while the FM one does not. Similarly, certain wavelengths of light get scattered by the molecular size of the gas and dust they strike, while others don't.

In the top image here, visible light from a nearby star (out of the image frame) reflects off the dust and gas, masking what is inside the cloud. When viewed in infrared light, however, the situation is different, and one can clearly see stars—and fascinating stellar jets—within the cloud.

The Lord "sees" everything. He is not hindered in His vision by day or night, clouds or Sun. He not only sees what we do, but He also sees into our hearts. He perceives our good intentions and worship, as well as our unbelief, vengeful motives, and stubborn lack of forgiveness. Our hearts are laid bare before Him, both in evil and in good. May this truth cause us to fear the Lord, humbly cling to Christ for the forgiveness of our sins, and seek the Spirit of God to help us purge our hearts of all evil.

If I say, "Surely the darkness shall fall on me,"
Even the night shall be light about me;
Indeed, the darkness shall not hide from You,
But the night shines as the day;
The darkness and the light are both alike to You.

Psalm 139:11–12

THIS COMPLEX AND REMARKABLY BEAUTIFUL CELESTIAL OBJECT IS KNOWN AS the Ant Nebula. Seen through small ground-based telescopes, its shape resembles the head and body of a common garden ant. Viewed through the Hubble Space Telescope, however, the sight is anything but common. Its odd shape and amazing intricacy are unique—and defy easy explanation. Most scientists agree that the central star of this nebula is near the end of its normal lifetime. Stars are immense and extremely complex energy sources. Nuclear fusion in a star's core produces an outward force that is counter-balanced by the downward gravitational weight of its outer gaseous layers. As the ratios of these forces change in a star over time, mathematical models predict that stars could implode or explode. Sometimes stars apparently blow off their outer layers, collapse, and then live to explode again. In the case of the Ant Nebula (also known as Menzel 3), multiple outgassings have pro-duced a very complex structure. The reason for its overall bipolar shape is not yet understood.

The basic message of our contemplation today is this: man's wisdom and understanding cannot even begin to compare with God's. What astronomers thought they knew about the causes of planetary nebulae like this one is now recognized as only a very small part of the complete picture. The confident scientists of yesterday are gone today. Are you intimidated by scholarly cri-tiques of your faith? Remember the words of Psalm 94:10–11: "He who teaches man knowledge—the LORD—knows the thoughts of man, that they are but a breath" (ESV). God is not manipulated or outsmarted. He has "cho-sen the foolish things of the world to put to shame the wise" (1 Corinthians 1:27). *He* teaches *us* knowledge. It was He who fashioned our brains in the first place! If you need wisdom, ask God for it. He's not like the overbearing teacher who makes you feel foolish for even asking a question. He gives wis-dom generously and without reproach (James 1:5).

Praise You, Lord, for Your great wisdom and for Your gracious promise to give it to us as well. May our boasting ever and only be in You, amen.

Where were you when I laid the earth's foundation?
Tell me, if you understand.
Who marked off its dimensions?
Surely you know!
Who stretched a measuring line across it? . . .
Do you know the laws of the heavens?
Can you set up God's dominion over the earth?

Job 38:4–5, 33 NIV

Man's *Miniscule* Knowledge

See, oh man, His hand of might;
Study here His glories bright;
Can you summon half this show?
What, oh man, now do you know?

THE SPRING CONSTELLATION HERCULES CELEBRATES THE mythical Roman demigod of the same name—who actually is patterned after the Greek figure Heracles. Both were men of extraordinary strength, courage, and ingenuity—yet given to help others. Heracles, in particular, was said by some to have "made the world safe for mankind" and to have been its "benefactor" by conquering various deadly foes. The constellation is nearly as large the Big Dipper, though slightly fainter. It is easily recognized by a keystone shape that marks the hero's torso.

Moving from myth to fact, the world indeed has a heavenly benefactor, Jesus Christ—who so changed history that our calendar itself is based upon the date of His birth. Christ was not a demigod—that is, half god and half man—rather he was fully God and fully man. The physical, emotional, and spiritual strength of Christ displayed at the cross defies human analysis and comparison. Rejected by men and crucified, He is indeed the capstone of faith, conquering man's most terrible foes: Satan, sin, and death. He is the only means for men to be saved. As you reflect on these things today, bless again the spiritual "Hercules" who lives forever beyond all comparison, the truest benefactor of men: the Lord Jesus Christ.

Nor is there salvation in any other, for there is no other name under heaven given among men by which we must be saved.

Acts 4:12

Christe, the Strong

They spit upon His meekness
And struck Him in the face.
Their floggers swung with hatred;
They stripped Him in disgrace:
Deep worked the Roman anger
That tortured Him, a Jew:
Yet this His contemplation:
"They know not what they do."

His people cheered "Hosanna,"
Then had Him crucified.
They freed corrupt Barabbas;
To sentence Him, they lied.
He hung outside their city,
Where leaders mocked Him too;
Yet this, the hurt He carried:
"I would have gathered you."

No angels came to help Him
When heaven on Him fell.
The devil tried to reach Him
Through every lie in hell.
Unthinkable the anguish
As Father crushed the Son,
Yet this His firm conviction:
"Thy will, not mine, be done."

No selfishness, no hatred,
No spitefulness was there.
No unbelief, no cursing,
No pity from despair.
One sinful thought, one failure,
And Love would not succeed.
The ransomed souls of hist'ry
Must His perfection plead.

If He had faltered even once,
In flames of hell would men abide.
Then ponder Christ and praise at length
The strength of Him there crucified.

EXPRESSLY UNIQUE

Broadcasting its odd mystique,
Beams this rectangle unique;
Manifesting God's great glory
Is His endless inventory.

The earth is full of Your possessions . . .
In which are innumerable teeming things,
Living things both small and great.

Psalm 104:24–25

Tucked between the bright, well-known constellations of Orion (the Hunter) and Canis Major (the Big Dog) is a faint constellation known as Monoceros, a Greek word for unicorn. Within this constellation is found one of the most curious and unique sights in the heavens: the Red Rectangle Nebula. This Hubble Space Telescope image reveals why it is so named. For reasons that simply aren't understood, gas from the central star is shooting outward and being illuminated in a complex X-shaped pattern forming the "corners" of a rectangle. Astronomers think the central star is actually not one but two stars orbiting one another very closely and surrounded by a dense torus of dust. One of the stars may emit jets—like beams from a lighthouse—swirling in such a way as to produce the strange and remarkable patterns seen. The Red Rectangle is called a *proto-planetary nebula*, and it is unarguably unique.

Today, let our hearts praise our incomparably creative God, who has made all things unique. For though stars can be put into categories based on their similarities, every star in the heavens is distinctly different. The planets and their moons are wonderfully diverse; no two comets are alike, nor snowflakes, nor people. God is so gloriously infinite in power and creativity that endless diversity is as natural to Him as it is impossibly supernatural to us.

Lord, we worship You as the God of endless creativity. Give us minds that appreciate creativity and can imitate You in its exercise. Oh, magnify the Lord, and let us exalt His Name together! Amen.

I have made the earth,
And created man on it.
I—My hands—stretched out the heavens,
And all their host I have commanded.

Isaiah 45:12

Discovery, *Diligence,* *& Chance*

Lord, I'm working very hard
To honor You today;
Strengthen me in diligence;
Establish me, I pray.
Please send forth Your timely help
To prosper all I do;
I want nothing more than this:
That others might find You.

THE PLANET NEPTUNE ORBITS OUTSIDE THE SIMILARLY SIZED PLANET URANUS. While it is slightly smaller than Uranus, it is also denser, making it more massive—that is, heavier. Neptune is a mysterious world. Because of its greater distance from the Sun, it receives only about 40 percent as much light and heat as Uranus, but its temperature is nearly the same. Some unknown source of internal heat is keeping it warmer than it otherwise should be. Surprisingly, and for reasons that are also obscure, Neptune has the fastest cloud speeds of any planet in the solar system—as high as 1,300 miles per hour!

The discovery of Neptune is an interesting tale of diligence and chance. Careful observations by French astronomer Alexis Bouvard showed discrepancies in the observed position of Uranus from that which was predicted. After Bouvard's death in 1843, Englishman John C. Adams and Frenchman Urbain Le Verrier independently used Bouvard's observations to calculate the position of a body whose gravitational influence would explain these discrepancies. Neither of them were met with enthusiasm from their colleagues to devote large amounts of telescope time to search for a mathematically predicted planet. Adams was asked for some clarifications by the Astronomer Royal, Sir George Airy. He drafted a reply but for some reason never sent it. Meanwhile, Le Verrier—a year after he had received a letter on a completely different subject from Berlin Observatory astronomer Johann Galle—did reply. He took the opportunity to appeal for Galle to look for the planet. A student at the observatory, Heinrich d'Arrest, suggested to Galle that a recently made map of that area of the sky could readily be used to look for any object that changed position—the telltale sign of a planet. Galle agreed, and they discovered Neptune that very night, September 23, 1846.

Luke records that the apostle Paul thoughtfully and diligently went out to a riverside in Philippi to meet and witness to those present. In this way, he chanced to meet Lydia, a successful businesswoman who discovered her Savior that day in hearing the gospel. She begged Paul and those with him to stay at her house. That day, the church in Philippi was born.

Whatever work you are engaged in today—whether raising children, earning money, performing ministry, or studying the heavens—work hard at it. God rewards the diligent, as the book of Proverbs makes clear. Whether you're young or old, He will bless and establish your efforts in surprising ways. Commit them to Him, and watch what He does.

Whatever you do, work heartily, as for the Lord and not for men, knowing that from the Lord you will receive the inheritance as your reward. You are serving the Lord Christ.

Colossians 3:23–24 ESV

ONE OF THE MOST STARTLING AND AWE-INSPIRING ASSERTIONS IN THE Bible is that the Lord created the universe *ex nihilo*, that is, out of nothing—and did so by simply commanding it to be. In Hebrews 11:3, we read: "By faith we understand that the universe was formed at God's command, so that what is seen was not made out of what was visible" (NIV). Thinking of this as we gaze at the globular star cluster Omega Centauri—and realizing that it is but one of literally billions of such clusters in the universe—takes our breath away and drives us to our knees. Omega Centauri is located about 15,800 light-years from Earth, and it contains several million stars. These stars, of course, are not just tiny dots, but are actually huge balls of high-temperature plasma. Our Sun itself is about 864,000 miles across—3½ times the distance from Earth to the Moon! It is truly beyond comprehension that God has such power and authority to simply speak these colossal systems into existence.

The Scriptures reveal that all three members of the Trinity were involved in the moment of creation. In one of the marvelous scriptural metaphors of the Godhead, we read that God the Father's mouth uttered a Word using His Breath, and so the universe was created. Can words come forth without a mouth? Can there be any utterance without the exhaling of breath? Can breath exist by itself? The obvious answer to all these questions is no. The power of the Word issued forth from the mouth of God with the breath of the Spirit to create the universe. The Godhead acted in unity of purpose, exercising a division of "responsibilities" that makes the wonder of the universe with all its star clusters pale in comparison to the marvel of His Being.

O God, we worship You. Who could ever describe You? Who can comprehend You? Who can grasp Your awesome power? Hallowed, hallowed be Thy Name!

By the word of the LORD the heavens were made,
and all the host of them by the breath of His mouth. . . .
Let all the earth fear the LORD;
Let all the inhabitants of the world stand in awe of Him.
For He spoke, and it was done;
He commanded, and it stood fast.

Psalm 33:6, 8–9

Triune
IN
Creation

How truly words cannot describe
The glories visible inside
This single cluster, let alone
The billions like it that are known.
And yet this glory can't compare
To that which seraphs only dare
To glimpse, the awesome Three-in-One,
Who spoke, and nature was begun.

THE TWINS

Double-astered joy of winter:
Gemini, the starry twins.
Ways to bring the Master pleasure:
Fearing God and trusting Him.

Behold, the eye of the LORD is on those who fear Him,
On those who hope in His mercy.

Psalm 33:18

Two stars of nearly the same brightness are found in the winter sky near Orion the Hunter. These are Castor and Pollux, twin stars marking the constellation of Gemini, the Twin Brothers. In Greek and Roman mythologies, the brothers shared the same mother but had different fathers—resulting in Castor being mortal and Pollux a god. The two lineages gave them many half-brothers as well, in a most unusual family tree! Under Roman rule at the time of Christ, the Twins were regarded as the patrons of sailors. In fact, the New Testament writer Luke notes in passing that the ship that carried the apostle Paul from the island of Malta to the present Italian mainland had the Twins as its figurehead. Castor is a complicated star system comprised of two double-stars in orbit about one another, with a third double-star tracking through space nearby. Pollux is a giant orange star, only thirty-four light-years distant. It is known to be orbited by a planet about twice the mass of Jupiter.

Have you ever asked yourself the question: *how can I please God?* While one could write volumes addressing this question, a pair of "scriptural twins" provides us with a succinct answer. They're two phrases that appear together repeatedly in the Bible when the topic is raised: to fear the Lord and to hope (trust) in His mercy. We fear the Lord by honoring Him as awe-inspiring God, by loving righteousness, and by hating evil (Proverbs 8:13). But to fully please Him, He also asks us to place our hope in Him, that is, to trust Him. As Hebrews 11:6 puts it, in order to draw near to Him, He requires that we believe that He mercifully and richly rewards those who do. May these simple but inspired scriptural "twins" guide your daily steps toward pleasing Him: to fear the Lord and to trust in His mercy.

The LORD takes pleasure in those
who fear Him,
In those who hope in His mercy.

Psalm 147:11

But without faith it is impossible to please Him, for he who comes to God must believe that He is, and that He is a rewarder of those who diligently seek Him.

Hebrews 11:6

Perhaps the heavens serve us in no better way than to help us understand the concept of infinity. Take any spot on the sky, even one that seems devoid of stars, and aim a telescope there. What you'll find, as in this Hubble image, are thousands upon thousands of galaxies as far as you can see. In fact, astronomers chose to target a spot for this exposure near the Big Dipper that was virtually barren to the naked eye. Each galaxy in this picture is comprised of billions upon billions of stars. The Milky Way Galaxy that we call home has approximately 200 billion stars. If you were to start right now tapping and counting once per second, it would take you eleven days to reach the paltry number of a million. To reach a billion, you'd have to count for thirty-two years! Therefore, to number the stars in our Milky Way Galaxy alone, you'd need to count for 6,400 years!

All this is to say nothing about the mind-numbing sizes and distances of these enormous celestial cities. Each galaxy in this picture is at least tens of thousands of light-years across. This means that at the speed of light—186,282 miles per *second*—it would take tens of thousands of years for starlight to cross from one side to the other! Again, using the Milky Way as an example, with a diameter of roughly 100,000 light-years, it spans 600,000 trillion miles!

Psalm 19 tells us that the heavens declare God's glory. They communicate His creativity, His power, His knowledge, and His majesty. But they also uniquely reveal His infinite, divine nature. He is so great that both islands and galaxies (sometimes called *island universes*) are like dust to Him. He scoops out the oceans with His hand and spins the galaxies with His finger! How could we ever begin to understand Him as the infinitely powerful Being that He is unless He set these things in place for us to see? But in His kindness, He did that very thing! God created the galaxies, the nebulae, and the very stars to help us know and trust Him. Does that change your perspective?

In Genesis we read that the creation of man was the high point of God's creative work. He cares more about us than about all the stars in the sky. By looking at the universe, you can either feel very, very insignificant—or very, very significant! Both are right. God would have us humbly worship Him as the great I AM and yet know that we are not cosmic accidents. We are the apple of His eye, the people He created for fellowship.

Let these wonderful truths carry you above the disappointments and troubles you face today. His plans for those who trust Him in Christ are as glorious as any He has for the stars. Give Him your worries and cares. He is not only infinite in being but infinite in love to those who fear Him (Psalm 103:11). He invites us to know Him both in His power and His love. King David knew God. In Psalm 62:11–12, he tells us, "One thing God has spoken, two things have I heard: that you, O God, are strong, and that you, O Lord, are loving" (NIV).

Who has measured the waters in the hollow of his hand,
or with the breadth of his hand marked off the heavens? . . .
Surely the nations are like a drop in a bucket
they are regarded as dust on the scales;
he weighs the islands as though they were fine dust.

Isaiah 40:12, 15 NIV

GOD'S INFINITY

The islands are as dust to Him;
Their swirling deep, His palm conferred.
Alike suspend the galaxies,
Concentered where His finger stirred.

The
Jewel Box

Treasure is where treasure does;
We're rich if we believe
Our happiness comes when we give
And not when we receive.

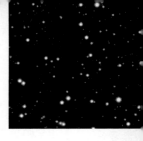

KEEN-EYED OBSERVERS IN THE SOUTHERN HEMISPHERE CAN detect that a star within the constellation of Crux, the Southern Cross, is not sharp, but hazy. Binoculars or a small telescope will reveal the reason why: the "star" Kappa Crucis is really an exquisite cluster of about a hundred stars. Reported first in the mid-eighteenth century by a French astronomer operating in what is now South Africa, it was later described by the famous English astronomer Sir John Herschel as "a casket of variously coloured precious stones." Hence it became known as the "Jewel Box." The cluster is located 6,440 light-years from Earth and is comprised primarily of brilliant blue-white stars. Embedded among them is a bright orange supergiant star, providing a lovely visual contrast with its companions.

Where is your "jewel box"? Is it in heaven? It should be. Jesus, speaking of His kingdom, told a parable about a man who found a treasure hidden in a field and sold all that he had to buy the field in order to gain it. Could this be said of you? Are your time, energy, and money spent on honoring the name of Christ and advancing His kingdom? If your heart and mind are not given to kingdom things, chances are your money is not there either. No doubt thinking of his Master's words, the apostle Peter admonishes us to rejoice—because through Christ, our living hope, we have "an inheritance incorruptible and undefiled and that does not fade away, reserved in heaven for you" (1 Peter 1:4). Christ's happiest saints are those who live generously and sow their wealth into heavenly things rather than simply acquiring earthly possessions.

Lord, help us to avoid the trap of materialism so that our fruitfulness is not choked out by the deceitfulness of riches and the desire for other things. May our lives be so Christ-oriented that our deepest delight is to give our lives away to see You glorified. In Jesus' name, amen.

"*Lay up for yourselves treasures in heaven, where neither moth nor rust destroys and where thieves do not break in and steal. For where your treasure is, there your heart will be also.*"

Matthew 6:20–21

And remember the words of the Lord Jesus, that He said, "It is more blessed to give than to receive."

Acts 20:35

Shine *by* His Glory

Blackened, lifeless, cold, and grim—
Such was my estate in sin.
Then the mighty Son drew me;
Hence I'll shine by His glory.

AN ASTRONOMER ONCE COMMENTED THAT THE TAIL OF A COMET IS "as close to nothing as you can be and still be something"! Pushed into space by the action of the solar wind, the tail of a comet can stretch thinly for millions of miles behind its icy nucleus. Comet nuclei are generally small—tens of miles long—and are comprised of a mixture of ice and soot that's no prettier than week-old snow on the side of a highway. Orbiting on highly elliptical paths, they spend most of their lives in the dark, bitter-cold of space—millions, if not billions, of miles from the Sun. It is only when they are drawn into the inner solar system by the Sun's gravity that they warm and out-gas tails. Vaporized off the comet's surface, a tail spreads its ugly "smoke" out so thinly that we would consider a sample of a comet's tail to be a fine vacuum here on Earth. In this image of the comet Hale-Bopp, two tails can be seen: a blue ion tail of fluorescing carbon monoxide and a yellow-white dust tail. It is the brilliant illumination of our yellow Sun that allows this dust tail to be seen at all against the jet-blackness of outer space.

Spiritually speaking, our lives are like that of the comet. Hopelessly darkened, with hearts as hard as ice, we lived far away from God and His grace. But then He drew us to Himself and brought the light of the gospel to bear on our souls so that we were transformed. Though nothing in and of ourselves, we now shine beautifully with the righteousness and glory that come from Christ.

Lord, how can we thank You enough for drawing us near and changing us forever by your grace? May our transformed lives daily reflect You—brilliantly and beautifully—for the whole universe to see. In Your holy name, amen.

Therefore remember that you . . . were without Christ, being aliens from the commonwealth of Israel and strangers from the covenants of promise, having no hope and without God in the world. But now in Christ Jesus you who once were far off have been brought near by the blood of Christ.

Ephesians 2:11–13

Complex Lives

What a mixture God must see;
Yet He loves remarkably.
Though our lives are tempest-tossed,
Jesus came to save the lost.

But God demonstrates His own love toward us, in that while we were still sinners, Christ died for us. Much more then, having now been justified by His blood, we shall be saved from wrath through Him. For if when we were enemies we were reconciled to God through the death of His Son, much more, having been reconciled, we shall be saved by His life.

Romans 5:8–10

THE TRIFID NEBULA IS A STUNNINGLY BEAUTIFUL REGION OF GAS, STARS, and dust located about 7,600 light-years from Earth in the direction of Sagittarius. Its name comes from the fact that it is comprised of three distinct types of nebulosities. The red portion is called an *emission nebula* since its glowing light is emitted by gas energized in the ultraviolet light from nearby stars—much the same way a neon light works. The blue portion is a *reflection nebula*, where gas and dust are not energized sufficiently to glow but simply reflect starlight—something like high clouds. The third type forms the dark lanes that are seen throughout. These are *dark nebulae*, comprised of larger and/or denser dust grains that block the light from behind them. The overall site is always changing as gravitational forces move the stars, which in turn swirl and illuminate the gas and dust in magnificent new patterns.

Our lives can be likened to a complex, ever-changing nebula like the Trifid. In our minds and hearts is a constantly changing mix of current knowledge, experience, misconception, and abstract truth. Love, fear, and pride act as forces that frame and shape our decision-making in both predictable and unpredictable ways. Perhaps today your soul is in a muddle. So much is happening around you with so many opinions and options that it's hard to know what to think or how to act. If that is the case, there is good news for you today: the Lord loves confused, fallen sinners.

In Mark 10:21, we read that Jesus looked with love upon the rich young ruler who was wrestling with which was more important: spiritual wealth or material wealth. In Luke 7, we read of how Jesus loved and defended the woman Scripture confirms was indeed a sinner when she anointed His feet in the house of Simon the Pharisee. Jesus even loved and protected His disciples in the Garden of Gethsemane after they had just failed Him in His greatest hour of need. While we're in the middle of what seems like a mixed-up mess, the Lord—by His grace and faithfulness—keeps a view of us that's like our view of the Trifid Nebula: complex, changing, mixed-up, messy . . . but beautiful.

Lord, we praise You yet again for Your amazing love, amen.

O LORD, how great are Your works!
Your thoughts are very deep.

Psalm 92:5

ONE OF THE UNINTENDED BUT GREAT TRAGEDIES OF OUR TIME IS THAT CITY lights and sprawling suburban eateries, shopping malls, and stadiums have so "polluted" the night sky with light that only the very brightest stars remain visible. Many adults have never seen a shooting star (a meteor), a comet, or even the Milky Way because of this light pollution. Man's insensitivity to this issue is akin to operating a smelly garbage-processing facility in the middle of a fragrant rose garden, or a smog-belching smokestack within a glorious national park. Fortunately, various groups have recently come together to reclaim what they can of the night sky by urging local officials to permit only downward-directed lighting within their municipalities.

A more general question should be examined, however: are we dull toward God because of all the man-made, technological, "gee-whiz" items at our disposal? In Mark 4:19, Jesus warned that "the desires for other things" chokes out God's Word. In 2 Timothy 4:10, we read Paul's mournful comment that "Demas has forsaken me, having loved this present world . . ." Let us soberly examine ourselves. Are we being so polluted by the man-made media around us—the movies, music, and video games—that we have no time to invest in knowing and loving the God-made things—nature, the Word, marriage, family, fellowship, and the church? May it never be! Instead, may the Lord develop in us a keen, deep longing to know more about the things He has made and what He is presently doing in the Earth. May we be enrolled on a front row seat in "Wonder University," daily marveling at and worshiping the God whose every thought and purpose is worth treasuring and studying.

Lord, thrill us again in "Wonder U" today!

Marvelous are Your works,
And that my soul knows very well.

Psalm 139:14

WONDER UNIVERSITY

Though men refine electric lights
That dull their sensibility,
I'd rather learn from starry nights
In "Wonder University."

How Awesome Is That Day to Me

How awesome is that day to me—
O day of hallowed history!
Set time in God's determined plan
To sacrifice the Son of Man.
What famous work that day was done
By Jesus Christ, His perfect Son!
The Second Adam, sent to save,
Humbly obeying to the grave!

How savage is that day to me—
O day of pure brutality!
When Christ, the Son of God Most High,
Was fiercely whipped and hung to die.
And oh, the horror of my sin,
Seen there in His appalling skin!
For God struck down—as meant for me—
The sinless One, at Calvary.

How precious is that day to me—
O day of purchased liberty!
In Him, a freeman now I live;
My sins, through death, did God forgive.
No wrath at length looms o'er my head,
But lovingkindness there instead.
His righteousness, my guilt replaced,
And Love, this ransomed soul embraced!

O awesome, savage, precious day—
'Tis God the Savior on display!
What peerless, holy, gracious Mind
Would fashion such a Grand Design?

Are you facing a hard day? Then please read on, for God wants to encourage you. Among the many deep and wonderful things to contemplate regarding Christ's Passion is that Jesus very likely read or sang Psalm 118 before heading to the Garden of Gethsemane. Psalm 118 is part of the traditional Jewish Passover celebration Jesus celebrated the night He was arrested. One can only imagine what was racing through His mind as He read "the stone that the builders rejected has become the cornerstone" (v. 22 ESV), "the LORD is on my side; I will not fear. What can man do to me?" (v. 6 ESV), "This is the gate of the LORD; the righteous shall enter through it" (v. 20 ESV), and "Bind the festal sacrifice with cords, up to the horns of the altar!" (v. 27 ESV).

But buried in the Psalm, and meant to give Him courage in that fateful hour, is this profession of astounding faith: "This is the day that the LORD has made; let us rejoice and be glad in it" (v. 24 ESV). Because Jesus knew that God the Father loved and was for Him, He was able to trust His Father and humbly obey His will—even unto death. God created that awesome, astronomical day just as He created today. If the Lord has made it and given it to us with the promise of His inseparable love, let us rejoice and be glad in it.

This is the day that the LORD has made;
let us rejoice and be glad in it.

Psalm 118:24 ESV

As we all know, life is complex. People aren't easy to understand; neither are pets, cars, or computers. Take almost anything really—like the weather—and try to fully predict, describe, or control it, and you'll quickly find that it's impossible! So it's understandable, though embarrassingly basic, that scientists cannot tell us what holds the physical universe together. "Gravity" is layman's answer—and this is correct—but what is gravity? What causes it? Why and how is it associated with matter? These are actually some of the top questions in the minds of twenty-first-century physicists.

The Standard Model of Particle Physics favors a thing called the "Higgs boson" (nicknamed the "God particle") to provide us with the answers. To give some background (meant only to humorously indicate how complex the problem is!), *bosons* are a distinct family of elementary particles separate from (but related to) the family of quarks (six each) and the three "generations" of leptons (electronic, muonic, and tauonic), each of which comes in the two "flavors" of particle and neutrino. The Higgs boson is one quantum component of the theoretical Higgs field, which gives empty space a "non-zero vacuum expectation value." The Higgs field itself consists of two neutral and two charged component fields. (Stay with me here!) Every elementary particle that couples to the Higgs field acquires mass through what is called the "Higgs mechanism," the breaking of electroweak gauge symmetry through the acquisition of a non-zero vacuum expectation value. Once a particle acquires mass, it can emanate a gravitational field that's mediated through gravitons. Make sense? *No, not really!*

Though there's surely some amazing God-given physically mediated means that makes it happen, the Bible gives us a simpler, more comforting answer that gets to the root cause: Jesus holds all things together. Hebrews 1:3 tells us, "He is the radiance of the glory of God and the exact imprint of his nature, and he upholds the universe by the word of his power" (ESV). If Jesus can hold the universe together, and if He is, in fact, doing that right now, don't you think He can hold your complicated life together too? Ask Him to give you eyes of faith to see that He both can and will. After all, He's holding your very atoms together right now—somehow!

For by him all things were created, in heaven and on earth, visible and invisible. . . . And in him all things hold together.

Colossians 1:16–17 ESV

Holding
It Together

No grand theories ever flower
Greater than God's Word of power.
Be they stars, or lives, or weather:
Lord, You hold them all together.

But although He had done so many signs before them,
they did not believe in Him, that the word of Isaiah the
prophet might be fulfilled, which he spoke:
"Lord, who has believed our report?
And to whom has the arm of the LORD been revealed?"

John 12:37–38

THIS EXQUISITE HUBBLE SPACE TELESCOPE IMAGE SHOWS ONE SPIRAL ARM of the magnificent galaxy called the "Southern Pinwheel," M83. It is located in the constellation Hydra and always appears low to the horizon for northern observers. Its bright, beautiful spiral arms wrap clear to its center, reminiscent of M101, the Pinwheel Galaxy, found much higher in the northern sky. Unlike other galaxies, and for reasons not completely understood, the core of M83 is ablaze with young star clusters. These clusters contain hot, blue-white stars that flood their surroundings with ultraviolet light. This light gets absorbed and re-emitted as red by interstellar material. The scale of the galaxy and its glorious arm are difficult to grasp. Astronomers estimate the galaxy to be 55,000 light-years across. This is roughly 330,000 *trillion* miles!

Scripture speaks of another glorious and mighty arm: Jesus, the Son of God, the arm of the Lord. This metaphor is used throughout the Old Testament and is mentioned too in the gospel of John. It indicates God in action—strong, purposeful, saving, and ruling. Jesus is strong and purposeful as God's agent in creation, He is saving at Calvary, and He is ruling forever in the kingdom. How fitting that we should think of Him as we gaze in wonder at M83's magnificent spiral arm. Even more than the galaxy could ever be, He is glorious, powerful, beautiful, and completely beyond comprehension.

Lord Jesus, receive our praise and worship yet again today. How we thrill to think of the day when we will see you face-to-face.

Behold, the Lord GOD shall come
with a strong hand,
And His arm shall rule for Him;
Behold, His reward is with Him,
And His work before Him.

Isaiah 40:10

Ah, Lord GOD! Behold,
You have made the heavens
and the earth by Your great
power and outstretched arm.
There is nothing too hard for
You.

Jeremiah 32:17

NASA, ESA, and The Hubble Heritage Team (STScI/AURA). Acknowledgment: R. O'Connell

The
Arm *of the* Lord

Glory? Yes, but not as grand.
Beauty? Sure, but near Him, bland.
Powerful? We all agree—
But Christ is King eternally.

Two
REVELATIONS

If I gaze into creation,
Or with care Your Word pursue,
This I gain as compensation:
There revealed is more of You.

"The heavens declare the glory of God; and the firmament shows His handiwork." These are the familiar opening words of Psalm 19. In the psalm, King David encourages us to consider how "night after night" the heavens "declare knowledge" of God. But what is this knowledge? Romans 1:20 helps us here by elaborating on two invisible attributes of God that are clearly understood by looking at creation: His eternal power and His divine nature. We all know that in examining the heavens, our spirits witness deep within us that something (or Someone) very different from us is being revealed. The grandeur and scope of creation, along with the great power of its elements, convince our hearts that a divine Being is at work. By examining nature we can also conclude that God loves beauty and diversity, that He is endlessly creative, and that He is unsearchably intelligent.

But only the first part of Psalm 19 deals with nature and the heavens. The second part is devoted to considering and praising the Word of God. Why are these placed together? It is because the Word is the second great means that God has given us to know more about Him. Theologians call the revelation that comes through nature "general revelation" and that which comes through the Word "special revelation." The Word reveals many, many more details about God to us than we can discern through creation alone. These details amplify His greatness, as we understand that He is not only eternally and divinely powerful, but also morally glorious and wondrously personal, gracious, and compassionate. Just looking at the qualities mentioned in Psalm 19, we learn that God is wise, pure, holy, righteous, and eminently desirable.

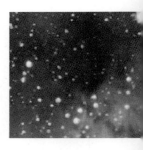

Today let us praise God for both His creation and His Word, realizing that through each of them God graciously chooses to reveal Himself and His loving intentions to us. And may we also act upon our knowledge and join David in seeking to please God in all we do, running to the Lord as our glorious "Strength" and our gracious "Redeemer."

Let the words of my mouth and the meditation of my heart
Be acceptable in Your sight,
O Lord, my strength and my Redeemer.

Psalm 19:14

*When the Lord saw her, He had compassion on her and
said to her, "Do not weep."*

Luke 7:13

THE BIG DIPPER—ALSO KNOWN AS URSA MAJOR, THE GREAT BEAR—IS ONE of the most recognizable of the constellations. Its "cup" of four stars is joined on one corner by a handle—bent in the middle—comprised of three stars. The middle star of the handle is named Mizar, an old Arabic name. Careful observers will note that Mizar has a tiny companion star nestled right beside it. Known as Alcor, this star is often regarded as a test for good eyesight, but even those with moderate vision can see it if they look closely. A small telescope reveals that Mizar is actually two stars. Larger telescopes equipped with spectroscopes show that each of those two stars is also binary, so four stars are tightly packed together. But Alcor is a binary star too! It appears to be revolving around a mutual center of gravity with Mizar. So all together they form an amazingly beautiful and intricate six-star system.

Insightful Bible teachers have distilled a beautiful principle from examining the life of Christ: "Love requires looking." See how often the Scriptures record that Jesus first "looked" or "saw" and then was moved to compassion. Are you too busy to look at those around you? God may have something amazing to show you. Slow down and begin to love the people around you by examining their situations and challenges. Maybe something that's hurt or "bent" will catch your eye. Looking carefully and lovingly will lead to compassion and then to action. So the next time you see the bent handle of the Big Dipper, be reminded to sharpen your gaze for tiny Alcor—and to look carefully and lovingly at those around you.

Lord, Your ways and Your Word are always filled with insight and truth. Help us to imitate Jesus in acts of compassion that begin with the look of love, amen.

*And when Jesus went out He saw a great
multitude; and He was moved with compassion for them, and healed their sick.*

Matthew 14:14

Looking
AND
Loving

Wonder starts with eyes that see
Both where bright and tiny be.
Learn this lesson from above:
Looking closely fosters love.

GOD
Unsearchable

In nothing is the mind more fully satisfied,
Nor does the eye or heart find rest,
More than in contemplating Thee.
And yet it is as if we skim the sheerest sprays
That blow across the broad expanse
Of some immense, uncharted sea.
Oh, drop the weight to fathom yet again His love,
And practice there with untold bliss
The soundings of eternity.

Oh, the depth of the riches both of the wisdom and knowledge of God! How unsearchable are His judgments and His ways past finding out! . . . For of Him and through Him and to Him are all things, to whom be glory forever. Amen.

Romans 11:33, 36

THE GREAT CARINA NEBULA IS LOCATED WITHIN OUR OWN MILKY WAY Galaxy, about 7,500 light-years distant. It is found in the southern constellation of Carina, the Ship's Keel. Recent Hubble Space Telescope images of its center stagger the mind with its beauty and complexity. In every corner of this vast interstellar complex are objects and processes that are each sufficient for lifetimes of study. Young, hot, radiating stars; fluorescing gases; dark, gaseous, silhouetting pillars; rushing stellar outbursts; gravitationally collapsing clouds; and galactic tidal forces all intermix to form an endless scientific paradise. Not to mention the fascinating, singularly massive, and volatile star Eta Carina—likely two or more stars itself—embedded in the middle of the nebula and ready to explode at any moment in a colossal supernova.

Considering this vast, glorious complex—whose intricacies are repeated a billion times over in other galaxies—turns our thoughts to the unimaginable greatness of God who made them all. Thinking of God and His infinite, detailed knowledge, King David exclaimed in Psalm 139:6: "Such knowledge is too wonderful for me; it is high, I cannot attain it." Psalm 145:3 says, "His greatness is unsearchable," and Psalm 147:5 adds, "his understanding is beyond measure" (ESV). Indeed, through His own gracious revelation of Himself, we can understand God in part, but we can never fully comprehend Him, or even a single one of His qualities. There will always be more of His wisdom to understand, more of His power, more of His holiness, more of His love. We will never fathom Him, and we will never tire of Him. Through all eternity, we will look upon Him and marvel at the endlessly creative, wonderfully gracious, uniquely righteous, timelessly beautiful, unsearchably glorious, infinitely loving Maker and Ruler of all.

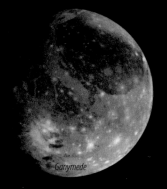
Ganymede

Io

And Isaac loved Esau
because he ate of his game,
but Rebekah loved Jacob.

Genesis 25:28

THE MIGHTY PLANET JUPITER HAS MORE THAN SIXTY CONFIRMED MOONS. BY FAR the largest of these are its four "Galilean" satellites—collectively named for Galileo Galilei who discovered them in 1610. These four—Ganymede, Callisto, Io, and Europa, from largest to smallest—are readily seen with even the smallest telescope and are favorite viewing targets for amateur astronomers. From Earth, the tiny starlike moons appear roughly the same size and brightness, and one would expect them to look similar if seen up close. Satellite views, however, show that they are remarkably different.

Io, the closest of the four to Jupiter, is the most geologically dynamic body in the solar system. It has over four hundred active volcanoes and is dotted with high mountains. In stark contrast, Europa—the next farther out—is one of the smoothest objects in the solar system, with very few craters but many strange crisscross markings. Its globe may be one huge ice rink that's frozen over an ocean of water. Ganymede, third distant from Jupiter, is the largest moon in the solar system—larger, in fact, than the planet Mercury! Its surface has ridges and craters of dark and light materials likely overlaying a subsurface ocean and an iron core. It is the only moon known to have its own magnetic field. Callisto is also large—99 percent the size of Mercury—but only having about one-third of its mass. It has one of the most heavily cratered surfaces in the solar system.

If you come from a large family, perhaps Jupiter's family reminds you of yours. Maybe you resemble each other from a distance, but up close you are each completely different. How often too that children born to the same set of parents are completely unique in personality and interests. Even identical twins aren't really identical! God loves variety, and He uses people's differences to build godly character within us. If you have very different siblings, children, or nieces and nephews, thank God for their diversity. Seek to love and encourage each person individually. This may cause you to spend more time on your knees in prayer, but good fruit will result. Think of the grief brought into the family of Isaac and Rebekah because they "played favorites" with their children. God forbid that this should occur with us!

Lord, praise You for the diversity in my family. Help me love each of them deeply and individually, just as You do, amen.

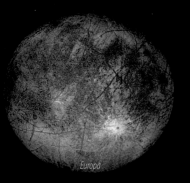

Europa

Callisto

*My brethren, do not hold
the faith of our Lord
Jesus Christ, the Lord of
glory, with partiality.*

James 2:1

Variety
BUILDS PIETY

Could there be four
That differ more?
Yet in each world—
Much to explore!
How verily
My family
Is much the same—
Uncannily!

195

Identity
Change

It's now no longer I who live,
But Christ who lives in me;
Attesting to this truth is that
My conduct well agree.
Lord, help me to replace the old
And practice now the new.
My keen, heartfelt desire is
That others might see You.

To the consternation of many, in 2006 the International Astronomical Union (IAU) "demoted" the planet Pluto to the status of a "dwarf planet." This was precipitated by the discovery over the previous decade of a large number of small icy objects located beyond the orbit of the planet Neptune—a band of small bodies known as the Kuiper Belt. The number of these objects known is now over 1,000. By virtue of its similar icy nature and location, Pluto is now considered by the IAU as a large Kuiper Belt object rather than a small, full-fledged planet. In a poor but perhaps helpful analogy, one might consider the solar system planets as various kinds of trucks ranging from small pickups to huge eighteen-wheelers. Imagine making the discovery that many very similar but different vehicles (cars) existed in numbers that greatly dwarfed the number of trucks. The IAU basically decided that Pluto should be called a large car rather than a small truck.

When a person becomes a Christian, their identity in Christ changes from an object of "wrath" to an object of "mercy" (Ephesians 2). Through faith, we are justified once and for all before God because of the saving work of His Son, Jesus, on the cross. Our pattern of living also necessarily changes, but not as instantaneously. We're taught later in Ephesians 4 to "put off" our old way of thinking and living and "put on" God's new way. Instead of stealing, give; instead of complaining, encourage; instead of hating, love. By "putting on Christ," we confirm our identity as one who's truly been changed from spiritual death to life.

Lord, help me to hate sin and to "put off" all those things associated with my previous worldly manner of living apart from You. Thank You for the new identity I have in Christ. What a miracle that this should have happened to me! May everyone who sees me know that I am truly changed and that I am Yours forever, amen.

Put off your old self, which belongs to your former manner of life and is corrupt through deceitful desires . . . and . . . put on the new self, created after the likeness of God in true righteousness and holiness.

Ephesians 4:22, 24 ESV

Do others find you easy to address or approach? Are you teachable? Do you listen well? Are you fulfilled by helping others, even doing behind-the-scenes work no one will notice? Do you consider others' interests more highly than your own? In short, are you truly humble, or are you proud? Pride is classified by theologians as the first of the seven "capital vices" or "cardinal sins." Indeed, its effects can destroy individuals, marriages, churches—even entire nations. We know from Scripture that it was this sin that caused Lucifer to be banished from heaven. In examining the details as recorded in Isaiah 14:12–15, we note that it was a sin of Lucifer's heart that God identified and judged, not any specific act or verbalized opinion. Let this truth cause a dose of healthy introspection within us today. God opposes the proud but gives grace to the humble.

We read too that Satan coveted sitting "on the farthest sides of the north" (Isaiah 14:13). What does this mean? Likely it means multiple things. For one, the ancients regarded the north as dark and obscure compared with the sunny south. Additionally, however, anyone who has spent significant time under the stars realizes that all the constellations move in large circles around Polaris, the "Pole" or North Star. This is because Earth rotates like a classroom globe about an imaginary shaft that runs through it, north to south. Timed exposures of the night sky taken due north—like the one here—clearly reveal this movement. Hence, "seated in the north" is another way of saying "the world revolves around you." Today let us examine our hearts soberly regarding this sin of pride. And let us repent if the Spirit of God convicts us of attitudes, words, or actions that are haughty, conceited, self-important, or arrogant.

How you are fallen from heaven,

O Lucifer, son of the morning!

How you are cut down to the ground,

You who weakened the nations!

For you have said in your heart:

"I will ascend into heaven,

I will exalt my throne above the stars of God;

I will also sit on the mount of the congregation

On the farthest sides of the north;

I will ascend above the heights of the clouds,

I will be like the Most High."

Yet you shall be brought down to Sheol,

To the lowest depths of the Pit.

Isaiah 14:12–15

PRIDE

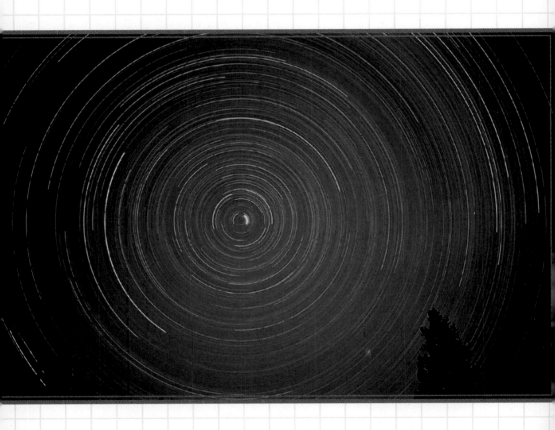

Is there pride within your soul,
Seated where it turns control?
Deadly is this carnal sin;
Through it, fallen worlds begin.

Can It Be?

Can it be that daily You
Return upon me smiling?
I would hardly look for You
Until the darkness falling
Caused an anxious glance to find
Your face, so reassuring;
Ever watching over me,
Thy grace, my soul securing.

—⁂—

Kevin Hartnett

Have you ever been startled to see the Moon during the day-time? Somehow it just doesn't seem "right" that it should be visible then. Isn't the Sun supposed to "rule the day" and the Moon "rule the night"? While these statements are unquestionably true, it is also true that as surely as Earth spins on its axis, our celestial companion, the Moon, appears at some time overhead during each twenty-four-hour period. We just don't notice it. Only for a day or so, on either side of what we call New Moon, is it found so close to the Sun that it can't be seen. Even the thin evening crescent Moon, which gets brighter and more noticeable after sunset, has been following the Sun across the sky all day. Once the Moon's phase progresses to First Quarter, it's brighter and quite obvious during daylight hours. Seeing it is more a matter of looking. If we're attentive, we can readily spot the Moon, day or night.

In Psalm 89, the Lord compares His faithful, covenant love to the ever-present Moon. He's faithfully watching over us whether we realize it or not, and His promises are as sure as the continued presence of the Sun, Moon, and stars in the sky. Do you seek the Lord only when darkness is setting in? He wants you to enjoy fellowship with Him at other times as well. Maybe you feel as though He's not thinking of you unless you're consciously spending time with Him. The Scriptures tells us otherwise. In 2 Corinthians 2:15 we read that "we are the aroma of Christ to God among those who are being saved and among those who are perishing" (esv). He is constantly aware of us—what we're thinking, what we're doing, what we're planning. He adopted us into His family at the cost of His own Son's blood. We are the apple of His eye (Psalm 17:8), His own chosen people (1 Peter 2:9), and a people for His own possession (Titus 2:14). By His grace, He's redeemed us, and He's not going to change His mind.

So the next time you see the Moon during the day or see the smiling evening crescent, pause and remember the timeless covenant God has made to love you and be your God. Then with all your heart, soul, mind, and strength, smile back at Him in loving worship.

My covenant I will not break,
Nor alter the word that has gone out of My lips. . . .
It shall be established forever like the moon,
Even like the faithful witness in the sky.

Psalm 89:34, 37

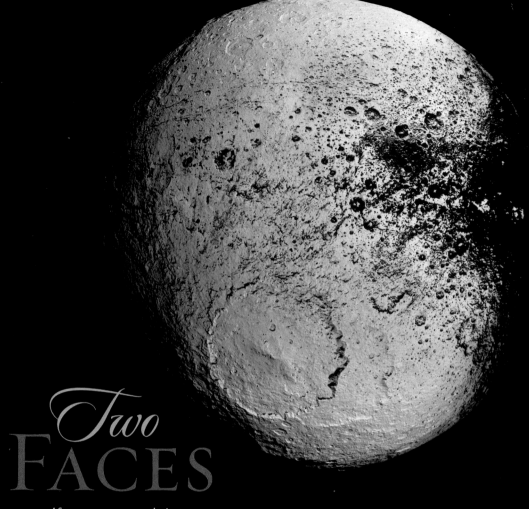

Two
FACES

If ever a complaint
Or thankless notion makes its way
Across my restless tonguè,
Or finds a haven where to prey
Upon my better sense,
May then the grace of God be plain,
Reminding me from whence
My soul's right destiny was claimed.

SATURN'S THIRD LARGEST MOON IS A CURIOUS BODY NAMED IAPETUS. Discovered in 1671, initially it could be seen only on one side of the planet! Astronomers correctly deduced at the time that its eastern and western hemispheres were very dissimilar in the way they reflect light. In fact, we now know that one hemisphere is white and the other a dark reddish brown. The best explanation for this two-faced world at present is that ice evaporates from the dark, warmer side and condenses out on the other side as bright, clean material. The dark side is left with an accumulation of some kind of soot that had originally been mixed with the ice.

When we are spiritually born again, our spirits become alive to God as new creations. Fresh, new desires to love Him and His kingdom result. But these are opposed by our old, carnal nature—though subordinate to the power of Christ now dwelling within us—which still tempts us and tries to drag us back to our old, sooty ways. We know that the mind set on the flesh leads to death and that the mind set on the Spirit brings life and peace (Romans 8:6), but many times the voice of the flesh shouts louder than the spirit, and we sin. What then? How do we grow in godliness?

God gives us many means of maturing—including His Word, His Spirit, prayer, fasting, fellowship, service, and self-denial. But an overarching thought is key: apart from God's mercy to us through Christ, our souls would be lost forever. In the unfathomable kindness of His grace, we who were dead, He made alive together with Christ (Ephesians 2). The voice of this truth is what should ring loudest in our ears! Knowing His grace makes us want more of Him—and less of anything else.

Likewise you also, reckon yourselves to be dead indeed to sin, but alive to God in Christ Jesus our Lord. . . . For sin shall not have dominion over you, for you are not under law but under grace.

Romans 6:11, 14

*S*TRETCHING MAJESTICALLY ACROSS THE GLOWING BAND OF THE SUMMER Milky Way is the large, strikingly beautiful asterism known as the Northern Cross. It forms the central section of the constellation Cygnus the Swan. The body of the Cross is easily recognized, as it extends down the Milky Way from the bright star Deneb at its top. The arms of the cross reach out to either side, marked by stars slightly dimmer than Deneb. At the foot of the Cross is Alberio, a beautiful two-color, telescopic binary star. As the sky rotates from summer to winter, the angle of the Milky Way with the horizon gradually changes. Many have noted that at the latitude of Jerusalem (about thirty degrees north of the equator), the foot of the Northern Cross just skirts the horizon so that in late December—near Christmas—the Cross appears to stand nearly straight up from Jerusalem's northwest horizon in the early evening.

If there was ever an event worthy of remembering and honoring some way in the stars, it is the crucifixion of Christ. There the transaction eternally planned by God to lovingly save sinners from His own justified wrath, and secure the justice that His own holiness demanded, was fully accomplished. In the most unbelievable and unimaginable exchange, the perfectly righteous Son of God consented to His own bloody execution so that we might go free. Our sins were laid upon Him, and He was sacrificed—just as pictured in the Old Testament sin offering of a male lamb without blemish. Our penalty was paid, God's wrath against us satisfied, our relational enmity with God reconciled, and our spiritual bondage and blindness because of sin lifted.

Whatever the problems you face today, if you have sincerely placed your faith in the saving work of Christ, God has already solved your most pressing need. No amount of penance, charitable works, or good intentions can ever remove the stain of sin from a soul. Only the blood of Christ can. Jesus poured it out graciously and freely on the Cross for those would believe. This is the gospel, the good news that will forever be proclaimed.

Then I looked, and I heard the voice of many angels around the throne, the living creatures, and the elders; and the number of them was ten thousand times ten thousand, and thousands of thousands, saying with a loud voice: "Worthy is the Lamb who was slain To receive power and riches and wisdom, And strength and honor and glory and blessing!"

Revelation 5:11–12

The
Magnificent Cross

O magnify the Lamb
Who bravely paid the price,
And walked the path alone
To brutal sacrifice.
His work commands the praise
Of all whose breath there be,
And shouts the grace of God
Into eternity.

Our Witness to the GENERATIONS

The stars I see are yesteryear's,
Their glow from flames of glory past.
And now my life, a light, appears;
How far will my effect be cast?

*I will sing of the mercies of the L*ORD *forever;*
With my mouth will I make known Your
faithfulness to all generations.

Psalm 89:1

IF YOU ENJOY STUDYING HISTORY, TAKE A WALK OUTSIDE SOME night and thoughtfully consider the stars. Quietly and beautifully, these colossal but remote celestial orbs broadcast information about the past. There's Sirius, the bright winter star, telling us things from eight-and-a-half years ago. Likewise see Vega—the brilliant summer star—whose transmissions come to us twenty-five years old. Rigel and Betelgeuse, the shimmering stars in the constellation of Orion the Hunter, tell us of things from nearly 1,000 years ago. These stellar history lessons are there because light doesn't travel instantaneously. It has a set speed. The stars are so immensely far away that their light takes years to span the vast abyss between us and them. Looking at the stars is truly experiencing the past. This is even more remarkable when one considers that the speed of light through the vacuum of space is 186,282 miles per *second*. This is nearly 6 *trillion* miles per year! At a distance of 93 million miles, even the Sun's light is eight minutes old! If the Sun were to go dark this instant, there'd still be eight minutes of light before we knew it!

Jesus taught us in Matthew 5 to be "salt" and "light." He said, "Let your light so shine before men, that they may see your good works and glorify your Father in heaven" (v. 16). How bright is your light? Will the generations to come still experience it? Stars are very different from one another, just as our Lord taught that some disciples bring forth fruit thirty, some sixty, and some even a hundredfold (Mark 4:20). Is your influence like that of a supergiant blue star or a faint white dwarf? Today, let's purpose with God's help to do all we can to make His mercies, faithfulness, and power known to our own generation and many more to come.

So even to old age and gray hairs,
O God, do not forsake me,
until I proclaim Your might to another generation,
Your power to all those to come.

Psalm 71:18 ESV

Are there really big issues facing you today? Does it feel like an emotional earthquake is happening and everything around you is shaking? If so, the Lord would speak a word of peace and hope to you from Psalm 46—especially if you're a woman. You see, there's a heading to the psalm that says it's a "song for Alamoth," that is, for female voices. The gist of the message is this: God is not removed from you or somehow "chased away" by the problems that rock you. No, God is very present—right in the middle of it all—and is your refuge, strength, and help.

A *refuge* means protection—from evil men, jealous or hateful coworkers, or others who might hurt you or damage your reputation. God protected David in the back of a cave while Saul (who was trying to kill him) was resting in the front!

Strength means courage and ability to function when you'd rather just emotionally collapse. Think of Mary and the strength she found to go to the tomb as soon as she could after Christ's burial. Strength comes as soon as you realize that He is with you and that His Spirit works to bring order in the middle of chaos. He will be exalted for His Name's sake as your Deliverer; do not fear.

And *help* means, well, help—provision, comfort, rest, and assistance in your difficulties. This may come through an unforeseen change of circumstances or through the intervention of another person. But note *when* the Lord promises to bring the help: "just at the break of dawn" (v. 5). Not late, not early, but just when it's needed. God made the universe to function in time, but He marvelously is not bound by it. He will not be late. So if your world is shaking, go to Psalm 46 today. Put your feet in the streams that make glad the city of God, even in the midst of all that is raging about you.

There is a river whose streams shall make glad the city of God,
The holy place of the tabernacle of the Most High.
God is in the midst of her, she shall not be moved;
God shall help her, just at the break of dawn.

Psalm 46:4–5

Just IN Time

Is there shaking in your life
That's causing you to quake?
God is in the midst of it:
And you, He'll not forsake.
Fear tempts you to worry, but
He'll strengthen you to wait;
Even though it's black outside,
His help will not be late.

CHRIST,
the Substance

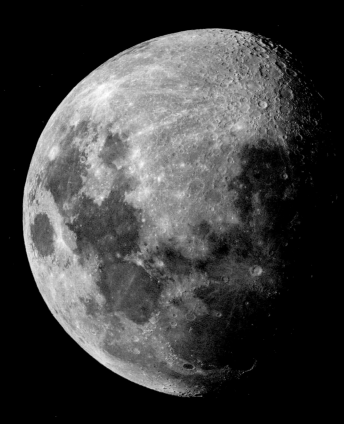

If you traveled to a foreign country
Purposing to save the one you loved,
Would you not desire their full attention?
So it is with us and Christ above.

Our celestial neighbor, the Moon, is visible in the sky because it reflects the light of the Sun. As it revolves around Earth, it presents differing phases of illumination to us as the geometry of the three bodies changes from night to night. When the Moon lies between us and the Sun (New Moon), it is invisible from Earth because its illuminated face cannot be seen from our angle of view. About two weeks later, when the Moon has revolved halfway around Earth (Full Moon), its fully lit face is pointed directly toward us. Two weeks more, and it's back to where it started twenty-nine days earlier, and the cycle repeats itself. Halfway between New Moon and Full is the First Quarter Phase, and halfway between Full and New Moon is the Third Quarter Phase. These obviously refer to how far the Moon has traveled around its orbit. Our culture bases its calendar on the Sun and Earth, so the Moon's phases shift slowly against the calendar dates. Other cultures time their calendars and holidays around the lunar cycle itself.

Writing to the Colossians, the apostle Paul urges them to never let religious things, whether foods, drinks, dates ("New Moons"), or festivals become substitutes for Christ Himself. How well this warning also applies to us! Things like attending a particular service, wearing certain vestments, or eating certain foods don't ultimately fulfill us or draw us closer to God. Christ Himself is the substance of our fulfillment. Knowing Him as our victorious Redeemer and grasping the love of God that planned our great salvation brings us assurance for daily living.

O Lord Jesus, please reveal more of Yourself to us. Help us see more clearly the riches of wisdom, knowledge, and love that are found in You. Thank You for the power of the gospel, which not only roots us in love, but also helps us live complete and fruitful lives—knowing, loving, and serving You.

So let no one judge you in food or in drink, or regarding a festival or a new moon or sabbaths, which are a shadow of things to come, but the substance is of Christ.

Colossians 2:16–17

The star Alpha Centauri is the third brightest star visible, but most people have never seen it. That is because the constellation Centauris is found in the skies of Earth's Southern Hemisphere. Alpha Centauri's main claim to fame is that it's the closest star to Earth, excluding the Sun. This is why it appears so bright. But some people will argue, saying they have learned that Proxima Centauri is the closest star. Many textbooks say this is so. So what's going on here? The truth is that both are right! Proxima is the faint red companion star of the much larger star, Alpha. Though separated on the sky from Alpha by the distance of more than four full moons, both are moving through space in the same direction and speed. It is assumed, therefore, that Proxima actually orbits Alpha, but on time-scales that make its orbital motion too small to detect. Proxima turns out (for now) to be closer than Alpha, but that could change with time as Proxima swings to the far side of its assumed orbit around Alpha. But wait! Alpha is really two stars, not one! Telescopes have revealed Alpha to have two close components: one yellow and slightly larger than the Sun, and one orange and slightly smaller. So if, in fact, Proxima is part of the system, Alpha Centauri is really three stars—a triple star system—all bound together gravitationally, though each distinct in its characteristics.

The Bible clearly teaches that there is one God comprised of three distinct Persons—Father, Son, and Spirit. Each Person has unique characteristics, yet together They are marvelously inseparable as one Deity. It is noteworthy and wonderful that the inspired Hebrew words used for God, *Elohim* and *Adonai*, are plural nouns but are used with singular verbs. A preacher once called God the "ultimate alien." How true this is! He is beyond human comprehension or description. How fitting that His revealed covenant name should simply be "I AM WHO I AM." Today, let us bow in adoration before our indescribable and glorious God: Father, Son, and Spirit.

Go therefore and make disciples of all the nations, baptizing them in the name of the Father and of the Son and of the Holy Spirit.

Matthew 28:19

THE Trinity

Note them three, but count them one—
Triple stars unlike the Sun.
Likewise God will always be
One in essence; yet as Three.

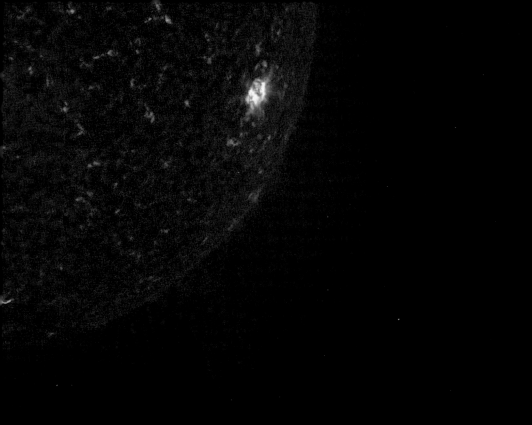

EARTHBOUND EYES

Earthbound eyes can e'er but see
Causes circumstantially.
Lift your eye to heaven's view:
He who forged the stars formed you.

IF YOU NEVER GAZED INTO THE HEAVENS, YOU'D CERTAINLY HAVE A distorted view of reality. Imagine living on Venus, where the skies are perpetually covered with thick clouds. You wouldn't know your planet orbited the Sun, that there were other planets, or that the Sun was a star in a universe with billions of other stars. Even on Earth we've learned some pretty basic things by looking up. In 1868, a spectroscopic view of the Sun taken during a solar eclipse revealed a new bright emission line. This line revealed the presence of a previously unknown element. It was named "helium" after the Greek word *helios*, for Sun. It wasn't detected on Earth until fourteen years later, but it is now known to be the second-most abundant element in the visible universe.

Since the heavens declare the glory of God, a humble study of them can increase our spiritual understanding, as well as our grasp of physical reality. Minds that are focused on small, temporal things miss the truth that an eternal and powerful Being fashioned the universe. Without this understanding, life can seem senseless and haphazard, a string of unrelated circumstances. But God is purposeful. He created the universe and us within it—both to bring Him glory and to share in its pleasures with Him. He designed the womb where we were physically conceived as part of His "very good" creation. He also designed the wondrous plan to send His own Son into the world—"born of a woman, born under the law" (Galatians 4:4)—to redeem us when sin had entered creation, spoiled it, and separated us from Him. God's wonderful purposes include you. Of all things, this might seem the most amazing and unlikely. But look up—it is fully consistent with His marvelous works displayed all around you. Believe in Him; pursue Him; trust Him.

This is what the LORD says—
your Redeemer, who formed you in the womb:
I am the LORD,
who has made all things,
who alone stretched out the heavens,
who spread out the earth by myself,
who foils the signs of false prophets and makes fools of diviners,
who overthrows the learning of the wise and turns it into nonsense.

Isaiah 44:24–25 NIV

Self-Sufficiency

Kevin Hartnett

Lord, make it plain—the vital truth
Of Your sustaining power;
I need my eyes enlightened thus
To You this very hour.
I live in self-sufficiency—
A lie that boasts a name—
And candy-coat idolatry
That robs You of acclaim.

In Job chapter 38, we read an interesting interchange between Job and the Lord regarding the nature of knowledge and power. Actually, it's more like a judge or prosecutor (the Lord) cross-examining Job to clarify for him (and us) how we, as finite creatures, compare with Him, the infinite Creator. Of course, there is no true comparison.

To God, man's thoughts are "but a breath" (Psalm 94:11 ESV), his days like "a passing shadow" (144:4 ESV), and his schemes for power, laughable (2:1-4). And while God can make springs flow in a desert, divide the sea to form a dry path, calm a storm with a word, or raise the dead to life, we in comparison, to quote Jesus Himself, "cannot make one hair [of our heads] white or black" (Matthew 5:36 ESV). We cannot even understand all the "ordinances of the heavens" (Job 38:33 ESV), much less enforce or change them. As inhabitants of Earth's surface, we are powerless observers of the seasonal constellations where the Sun, Moon, and planets appear—in Hebrew, the *Mazaroth*. And instead of studying them with hearts full of worship to God, we err as societies by looking to them for personal guidance through the pseudoscience of astrology.

Have you ever confessed the sin of self-sufficiency? While this can mean independence from others that impedes the right functioning of the church, we also frequently mean by it that we're not thinking of God, seeking Him for strength, or looking to Him for wisdom. Today's thought is this: self-sufficiency is a euphemism for idolatry. The term self-sufficiency candy-coats a serious condition of spiritual blindness—for apart from Him, says Jesus, we can do nothing. Our very next breath depends on Him, our next heartbeat, our next thought. We're *not* self-sufficient. And if we're not daily seeking His power, marveling at His grace, or asking His Spirit for guidance, then our worship is going elsewhere.

O Lord, forgive our self-sufficiency, which really is a lie. Receive our worship afresh today. And may those around us see Your Holy Spirit working through our genuinely humble hearts. In Jesus' name, amen.

> *Can you bind the cluster of the Pleiades,*
> *Or loose the belt of Orion?*
> *Can you bring out Mazzaroth in its season?*
> *Or can you guide the Great Bear with its cubs?*
> *Do you know the ordinances of the heavens?*
> *Can you set their dominion over the earth?*
>
> Job 38:31–33

THIS BRIGHT METEOR WAS CAUGHT BY THE CAMERA AS IT SLASHED through the constellation of Cassiopeia, the Queen. Usually no larger than tiny pebbles, meteors, or "shooting stars," are bits of interplanetary material that vaporize many miles up due to interaction with Earth's atmosphere. Some of these particles are the outgassed debris from comets. Meteors enter our atmosphere at phenomenal speeds—some as high as forty-four miles per second. As they slam into the atmosphere, they produce a shock wave that rapidly heats the air around them to thousands of degrees Fahrenheit. This heat vaporizes the meteor, causing it to glow briefly, along with any ionized atmospheric gases along its path. Without our protective blanket of air, Earth would be subject to continual bombardment from meteors. During the particularly heavy 1999 Leonid Meteor Shower, amateur astronomers using telescopes equipped with video cameras captured the impact of several meteors into the airless surface of the Moon. If a meteoroid entering our atmosphere is large enough, a portion may survive its fiery descent and strike the ground. Such stones, called *meteorites*, are found all over Earth, but are particularly visible when strewn across the cold, white wastelands of the Antarctic.

In the Scriptures, there are many metaphors about the brevity of life: a flower, a dream, a blade of grass, a shadow. These contrast with the everlasting nature of God and should rightly produce humility in our souls before Him. But they should also inspire us to make the most of our short lives.

Is there someone nearby who needs encouragment with loving words or help? Are there important words to be said or actions to be taken that keep getting pushed aside? Don't let the frantic pace of life deter you from these important things. Like the meteor, we get no second chance to make an impact with our lives.

Lord, help us make a glorious mark for You.

O LORD, make me know my end
and what is the measure of my days;
let me know how fleeting I am!

Psalm 39:4 ESV

Fleeting Lives

Behold the fleeting meteor:
His life so short, his flame so bright.
He brings no second stroke to make
His mark against the fallen night.

Truth
AND Sacrifice

God, my Joy, Your truth has set me free;
How horrific that my life could ever be
Slave to devils' lies or schemes of men . . .
O Lord, receive my sacrifice of thanks again.

There's a fascinating story behind one of the fainter constellations of the Northern Hemisphere's spring sky. The constellation is called Coma Berenices, or "Berenice's Hair." It is named after the true-life historical figure of Queen Berenice II, the newlywed wife of Ptolemy III Euergetes, who reigned over Egypt from 246–221 BC. According to the story, Berenice swore to sacrifice her long blond hair to the goddess Aphrodite if her husband returned home safely from what historians now call the Third Syrian War. These were wars between the Seleucid Empire and the Ptolemaic Kingdom. Ptolemy III was successful, and upon his return to Egypt, Berenice kept her vow. But somehow, her hair was stolen in the night. To pacify the furious ruling couple, the court astronomer Conon of Samos (a truly accomplished Greek mathematician and astronomer), concocted the story that the goddess was so pleased with the sacrifice that she took the hair and placed it among the stars.

How wonderful it is that we as Christians live free from the pagan myths, superstitions, and fears associated with false gods. Jesus is "the way, the truth, and the life" (John 14:6). He told us that we would know the truth and the truth would set us free. Take time today from all the busyness that faces you to thank the Lord for setting you free—from Satan's lies, from the hopeless philosophies of men, from bondage to sin, from fear of death and judgment, from fear of God Himself. Our spiritual sacrifices are not hair, blood, or children. God delights in the sacrifice of thanksgiving (Psalm 50:14), a broken and contrite heart (51:17), and the worship of our everyday living (Romans 12:1).

For You do not desire sacrifice, or else I would give it;
You do not delight in burnt offering.
The sacrifices of God are a broken spirit,
A broken and a contrite heart—
These, O God, You will not despise.

Psalm 51:16–17

HE IS THE *Lord*

Stand up and bless the LORD your God from everlasting to everlasting. Blessed be your glorious name, which is exalted above all blessing and praise.

You are the LORD, you alone. You have made heaven, the heaven of heavens, with all their host, the earth and all that is on it, the seas and all that is in them; and you preserve all of them; and the host of heaven worships you. You are the LORD .

Nehemiah 9:5–7 ESV

THERE IS NOTHING GREATER OR MORE DESIRABLE THAN GOD—NO person, thing, idea, dream, or hope. The wonders of creation in the sky above and Earth below—in all their diversity, majesty, power, sophistication, elegance, and beauty—have poured out from the Lord as the profound words of a uniquely divine Orator. Everything wonderful and praiseworthy in the universe was His idea, spoken into existence by His incomparable almighty Being. At the end of the Age, on His great Day, every knee will bow and every tongue confess that He is Lord. Even now His astounded creation worships Him—the seraphim who fly around His throne, the great army of His redeemed from every tongue and tribe, the trees of the field, the fish in the seas, even the very rocks here groan and cry out His praise. But His name—His great name—the I AM THAT I AM—is exalted above all blessing and praise.

Today as you read this, bend the knee of your soul and worship Him. Nothing pleases Him more; nothing in your day is as right for you to do. He is the Lord.

Imagine all the wonders that abound
In ev'ry distant swirling galaxy,
That daily now in telescopes are found
As far as swelling apertures can see!
O think upon the splendid vistas there,
Where colored triple stars o'er planets rise,
While shining moons and rings their splendors share
With asters strewn 'cross bright galactic skies!
Will heaven then surpassing wonders show—
When God creates the universe anew—
And there, as promised, on His works bestow
A beauty He will never need renew?

Yes this shall happen, yet my soul must say:
One look at Him will sweep them all away.

KEVIN HARTNETT studied physics and astronomy at the University of Delaware. He lives with his wife of 30 years and their two children in the Maryland suburbs of Washington DC. A small group leader in his church for over 20 years, he has also written Christian poetry and song lyrics for more than a decade. Kevin has worked for 30 years at the NASA Goddard Space Flight Center supporting various aspects of satellite operations. He is currently NASA's Deputy Science Operations Manager for the Hubble Space Telescope.